In through the front door

14

Disabled People and the Visual Arts: Examples of Good Practice

Front cover: Carved Door by Keith Alexander, Avenues House Project, Gateshead Photograph: Barrie Houghton, Powerhouse Photography
Distributed by AN Publications, Freepost, PO Box 23, Sunderland, SR1 1BR. Telephone: 091 567 3589
Published by The Arts Council of Great Britain
Typeset by Home Office
Designed by Karen Felman
Printed by Staples Printers Ltd
Copyright © The Arts Council of Great Britain, Jayne Earnscliffe
ISBN 0-7287-0649-0

Also available on tape from: AIRS, Gateshead Central Library, Prince Consort Road, Gateshead NE8 4LN (091-477 3478)

contents

foreword

Over the last decade or so disability has come very much to the fore as both a political and a cultural issue. Having been essentially a taboo subject for many years this 'coming out' has been fraught with difficulties – laden with guilt, ignorance, anger, embarrassment and the like. It is in this context that people have worked with varying degrees of success to fill the gaps, gaps created by an assumption that disabilities debar people from being considered serious as either producers or consumers of art.

As an artist and a disabled man I have been both a participant in and an observer of this process. This book is to me particularly welcome because it looks beyond theoretical 'politically correct' approaches to disability. It concentrates on what has been achieved and how. The projects and organisations detailed here have explored a great variety of approaches. I regard this diversity as a key strength, there is no one right way of doing things.

The information contained in this book, however, points to many ways forward and should help avoid many pitfalls. If the visual arts world can build on the successes of the last few years it seems clear that this will not only benefit many disabled people but will enrich the culture as a whole.

Adam Reynolds 1992

Jayne Earnscliffe

Following careers in teaching and nursing, and a year at Queen Elizabeth Training College for the Disabled in Leatherhead, Surrey, Jayne Earnscliffe trained in arts management at the Whitechapel Art Gallery, east London, an opportunity created for a disabled person by the Arts Council and Shape London, where she was able to pursue her keen and active interest in the visual arts.

As a freelance consultant she now advises arts organisations on access, training and programming, and has had a number of related articles, reviews and exhibition guides published. In addition, she manages Artists First, a public art agency that commissions disabled artists, and sits on the London council of management of Shape. Jayne is currently training as a Disability Equality Trainer and continues to practise her own artwork.

introduction

By the year 2000, it is estimated that 50 per cent of the population of Europe may be disabled in some way,[1] partly due to its increasingly ageing nature. The situation today for disabled people wishing to enjoy the arts, both as consumers and practitioners, remains far from perfect and much needs to be done before the end of this millennium if that 50 per cent is not to be alienated from cultural life.

Access to the arts is a human right, yet prohibitive practices and barriers – physical, social and attitudinal – continue to prevent disabled people from fully and freely participating in them. With a surge in demand for greater access and equality of opportunity – partly brought about by the raised political consciousness and collective political clout of disabled people – service providers, funders and some politicians have recognised the urgent need for proper consultation, resourcing and legislation.

In response to this, a number of schemes and policies have already been instituted such as the ADAPT fund for adaptations to premises, Disability Equality and Awareness Training for arts employees, codes of practice on disability for galleries and museums, recently revised building regulations, and employment and training initiatives. All of these are intended to encourage employers in the arts to end discriminatory practice and to consider disabled people in every area of their work.

Improvements so far implemented in mainstream art venues have resulted in higher attendance figures across the social spectrum — which means increased revenues — and enhanced standards and services which have benefited everyone. However, many of the changes have come about through the initiative and perseverance of a few individuals, rather than as the result of policies based on recognition of need. The opposite is true of community-based projects and the disability arts movement, where user-led services have been created in direct response to needs and gaps in mainstream provision, and by the assertion of the right to representation.

The disability arts movement has been a cogent force over recent years, instrumental in effecting change nationally through raising awareness of disability issues, and by increasing the visibility and status of disabled people.

In order to write this book I travelled throughout Britain, visiting mainstream arts venues, disabled people's organisations, non-building-based projects and community initiatives. Thus, I experienced at first-hand existing and developing opportunities for disabled people.

Initially, the findings of my research were to have been presented as a list of examples of good practice. The idea for a book evolved from a recognised need to facilitate networking between the many organisations found to be working in isolation. The result is not intended as a definitive guide nor a panacea. *In Through the Front Door* contains six chapters covering topics which range from programming to employment. The chapters have then been sub-divided, giving a selection of case studies, good examples and initiatives that readers can examine as they need or wish to. I hope these will ignite the imagination and stir the conscience of all those who have yet to take action against oppression and prejudice, and acknowledge the achievements of some of those who already have.

Terms used throughout are disabled people's preferred terms at the time of going to print. They are based on the social (rather than the medical) definition of disability, which argues that it is environmental barriers and social attitudes that disable us. It is not the inability to walk, for instance, but the steps into a building that disable us.

---

[1] Frans Schouten, director of the Faculty of Museum Studies, Reinwardt Academy, Leiden, Holland, from *Museums Without Barriers* (pub. Routledge)

Standing alone running life's solitary risk but free,
Loosened from man's stifling, clamping kindness
No longer subject to the cutting edge of the groomed professional
Whittling one down to fit a category.
Gladly I resurrect the milestones of my destiny
Hoarding the boring, normal past
But setting it alight with candles of my chequered singularity.

Priscilla Judd CRAB, 1991

1 a change of programme

switching channels

Many disabled people wishing to participate in mainstream arts want them made more accessible through new means. "Touch" and multi-sensory exhibitions are becoming a regular feature of mainstream gallery programming as they make the art exhibited more accessible not just to disabled people, but to all visitors. These exhibitions can be fun while also being educational, challenging the way people interpret art. They also demand new aesthetics from artists, extending and enhancing their practice and understanding of art and communication.

There are a multiplicity of approaches to programming and no exclusive claims can be made for any one. The success of any exhibition rests on a combination of:

- exciting, high quality artwork which engages the imagination
- good physical access and presentation (including labelling and enhanced lighting)
- touch facilities
- tape commentaries (essential for independent exploration and orientation)
- information in accessible formats

Greenwich Citizens Gallery, London

This gallery is a fully accessible contemporary art venue with a commitment to presenting work by and for marginalised sections of the community. Its shop-front window looks out on to the high street of Woolwich enticing the public in.

Late in 1989, Barbara Hunt curated *It Makes Sense: Art Works to Touch, Smell, See and Hear*. This mixed-media exhibition comprised work by five commissioned artists and was aimed at encouraging the use of all the senses in enjoying and understanding art through full participation with the work. The overriding intention of the show was to question the assumed supremacy of sight over the other senses, and to increase access to galleries for disabled people by promoting awareness and debate on the issues surrounding disability.

It Makes Sense strove to move away from standard "touch" exhibitions by offering a variety of different stimuli including smell and sound to emphasise the interlinking of the senses in creating an overall impression of a work of art.

The gallery consulted widely with "touch" exhibition organisers, disabled art consultants, the Royal National Institute for the Blind, artists and the public. All agreed that the exhibition should be fully accessible to ensure that it would be both safe and easy for wheelchair users and visually impaired people to visit unguided, with all labelling and signage, positioning and work offering equality of experience.

The art on show included installations to walk through and art to smell, touch and listen to. One installation entitled *Cardboard City* was created by

pupils from local primary and disabled children's schools in conjunction with artists Jan O'Highway and Allan Davies. Workshops and demonstrations also took place throughout the course of the exhibition.

Litework of Morecambe, designers of light and sound units for people with sensory impairments, worked with *It Makes Sense*. Their contribution comprised fibre-optic products and optical kinetics such as bubble machines, mirror balls, touch and sound light boxes, motorised prisms, and "plasmadome", a crystal ball with streaks of blue and orange light which responded to touch and sound.

Lois Williams used household objects and "rubble of the past" to suggest half-forgotten memories. Sculptures, woodcuts and woodblocks by Tsugumi Ota could be appreciated by visually impaired visitors who had some residual sight. An installation by Karen Rann comprised netting,

Cardwell Primary School pupil during *It Makes Sense*

paper and elastic, and could be viewed from outside, within and below.

Conversation Peace (sic), an electro-sculpture by Ken Gray, exemplified technology that had been "humanised". An installation which invited interaction, it responded to the subtlest of human intervention — even a breath or the merest touch translated the stimuli into a babble of voices in eight different languages.

To advertise and promote the exhibition publicity material was sent to television and radio stations and newspapers. This resulted in extensive coverage, including an interview on German radio. All talking newspapers in London and surrounding counties were targeted, in addition to disabled people's organisations and journals. Large print and braille invitations and catalogues were also produced (see page 18).

Consultation with local groups of disabled people and full discussion of the exhibition with visitors provided valuable feedback to ascertain whether aims had been met and to identify any problem areas. This feedback confirmed that *It Makes Sense* had succeeded in reaching new audiences and in breaking down barriers both to the enjoyment of contemporary art and to physical access to a contemporary gallery and exhibition. *It Makes Sense* was one of the gallery's most successful exhibitions, attracting record attendances, including visits from over 40 schools and day centres.

Following on from this success a second multi-sensory exhibition was planned for January–April 1992. *BP re-Vision*, sponsored by British Petroleum and with support from the Arts Council, London Arts Board and Greenwich Council, sought to increase awareness and debate on issues of access and equal opportunities by providing a role model. The aim was also to directly involve those to whom the exhibition was geared — people with visual impairments — both as consultants and as artists.

BP re-Vision was unique in that it took the standard format of multi-sensory shows a step further by departing from the practice of using only

Visitor (and dog) enjoying straw chair from *Tables of Content* by apc, part of *BP re-Vision*. Photograph: Simon Pythian

Left: *Charles, a Gargoyle* (1988) by Adam Reynolds, from *BP re-Vision* catalogue Photograph: Gordon Cooper

three-dimensional, largely figurative art forms and including two-dimensional abstract forms. This mixed-media exhibition, like *It Makes Sense*, provided opportunities to explore contemporary art on a number of levels through active participation, encouraging new ways of looking based on the use of all the senses. But *BP re-Vision* was yet more challenging, demanding more critical enquiry.

As a starting point, a one-day seminar for artists making work for the exhibition was held in March 1991. This provided an opportunity for exhibiting artists to meet blind and visually impaired artists, critics and consultants, in order to discuss ways in which they could make work which would be accessible to them.

Work was commissioned from five artists, among them Marion Coutts who produced a hanging wall of slate entitled *Chime*, which – as its name suggests – could be played as a musical instrument. *Light Cave* by Jan O'Highway and sponsored by Litework was a black shell construction covered in fleeces, rocks and shells, aglow with gently pulsating fibre-optic lights contained within. Blind artist Flavio Titolo developed a new tactile aesthetic with his low-level plaster reliefs. A carved caramel sculpture by Yvette Thelermont, with its constantly changing surface and form, appealed to the olfactory sense. An art collective called apc created an environment which was likened to a "wrap-around outing for all the senses".

The exhibition catalogue contained essays exploring different issues around art and disability from disabled art practitioners and consultants. Artists' statements offered clues to their own work. Spiral-bound and illustrated throughout, the catalogue incorporated acetate sheets of braille text overlaying large print. Similarly, the labelling of all exhibits combined braille and large print presented on stands at wheelchair accessible height. To aid orientation, a tactile relief map of the gallery space and tape guides to the exhibits were available at the entrance.

Disability Awareness Training days were organised for staff of Greenwich Council throughout the course of the exhibition as part of a programme of review of service provision and access to venues in the borough. A disability sub-committee was also established, with representatives from all directorates, including housing, planning and social services.

BP re-Vision ran in conjunction with the Greenwich Women's Film Week, a performance of *Drowning* by the Black Mime Theatre, sculptural cooking demonstrations by Bobby Baker, described as "deliciously batty" and *Bloop*, "a special adventure" for children created by Theatre Venture for integrated deaf and hearing audiences and featuring a spaceship packed with "extraterrestrial things to do and see". All events were held at Greenwich Citizens Gallery to complement the exhibition and involve audiences further.

Other events organised around *BP re-Vision* included a movement and dance course for disabled people, and *Hound* by blind writer Maria Oshodi, performed by GRAEAE Theatre Company, Britain's leading professional theatre company of disabled people.

Audrey Barker/Kendal Museum, Cumbria

Audrey Barker is a disabled visual artist who has lived and worked in Cumbria for 30 years and exhibited widely. Specialising in participatory multi-sensory installations, she often introduces art into

Installation by Audrey Barker, *Festival of the Five Senses*

non-art settings such as leisure and shopping centres thus attracting large audiences. Using the tools and language of disability, i.e. braille, signing, raised print, as her art form, Barker describes her work as being popular without being populist.

Her practical commitment to arts and disability began in the 1970s with the founding of a sheltered arts/crafts workshop. This was developed into the Mill Arts Centre, Lanercost (1983–87). The centre was custom-built and the only one of its kind in the country in that it was organised and staffed by disabled people for the use of all the general public.

Theatre of Didactic Observance. Barker believes it is essential to engage the visitor by the most effective means possible, which entails working with carefully selected artists and performers.

Redesigned for the Shipley Art Gallery, Gateshead, *Another Way of Seeing* was later enlarged and extended for the Laing Art Gallery, Newcastle, where it attracted 18,000 visitors. The installation was modified to suit the needs and nature of each venue. Flexible in substance and ideas, it always remained an artwork in its own right. Accompanying performances were appropriately developed and expanded.

Apple Piece by John Joekes forms a core of activity in *Another Way of Seeing*

Festival of the Five Senses. **Photograph: Keith Pattison**

Knowing that the centre would have to close, Barker devised *Another Way of Seeing*, a sculptural exhibition suitable for touring. It was hoped that this project would extend and develop the philosophy behind the work promoted at Abbey Mill. The exhibition was intended to stimulate and expand awareness of the five senses. It introduced new ways of seeing everyday objects, and through its art content aimed to persuade the public into a general understanding of impairment and disability.

Another Way of Seeing was first commissioned for the Bradford Art of Disability festival in September 1987, to open the new Community Arts Centre. It comprised a multi-sensory participatory installation, and a specially devised performance, *Look, No Hands*, by the

The project was opened out into *The Festival of the Five Senses* for Wentworth Leisure Centre, Hexham, Northumberland (1989) where the exterior of the building, the adjacent supermarket, running track and indoor bowls hall all became part of the installation. This time, Barker commissioned works and workshops by sculptors, poets and performers from all over the country, a number of whom were disabled.

Whereas at Hexham the predominant theme was sporting activity, when it moved to the Natural History Museum, Kendal, ecological ideas were explored. Shown during May and June 1990, with financial assistance from the Scott Trust, Northern Arts, the Arts Council and Cumbria County Council, it comprised three site-specific installations based on the natural history elements of the museum.

Again, a new performance piece was commissioned by Barker, this time from Dr George Dodd from the Department of Olfactory Science, University of Warwick, who had also appeared at Hexham.

The Kendal project was devised and implemented in an entirely different way. Due to change in policy, Northern Shape (now Equal Arts, see page 77), which had successfully organised the event at Hexham, was no longer involved. Thus, the planning and execution of the event devolved directly onto the shoulders of the museum staff and the artist, as did fundraising.

This direct and constant consultation allowed for careful long-term targeting of publicity and information, and a healthy exchange of ideas between both parties. Once the exhibition began to take shape, staff overcame any misgivings about an enterprise so different from anything they had undertaken before.

Visitors were invited to participate in various activities which explored the five senses using sound, smell and tactile exhibits. These were housed in two of the museum's galleries, in its forecourt and garden. Five enormous banners with clear signage were hung outside the museum. Although artworks in their own right, they served to advertise the exhibition. A large-print guide to the work was produced and, as at Hexham, hanging signs in very large print and braille were distributed throughout the installation. A temporary ramp leading into the wildlife gallery and adapted toilet were provided to ensure disabled people were not excluded from visiting.

The title, *Another Way of Seeing*, was chosen to convey the many layers of meaning in the artwork, and the ways in which everyday objects can be discovered to be works of art, and everyday actions — such as dressing, seeing and listening — can each become small performances.

The wildlife gallery housed large glass-fronted show cases containing tableaux of animals, birds and butterflies. A cluster of these cases formed a centre island with other cases around the edge of the room. Above them were rows of stuffed animal

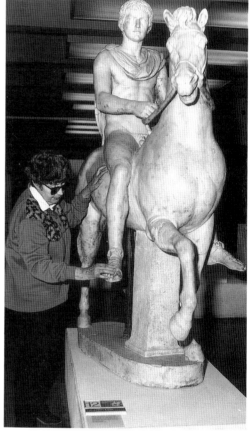

heads and every case and surface was covered in a filmy white material with peepholes cut at various levels to redefine the exhibits within. The stuffed heads became part of these white walls by careful use of draping. The contrast between the green carpet and the white drapes allowed for a clearly defined path around the exhibit from the entrance to the exit.

Overhead, and on either side of the path, were many tactile, aural, olfactory, visual and edible experiences. Revolving fans caused feathers and bells to flutter and sway, a loop tape played noises of insects, interspersed with snatches of "Up the Amazon", a comic song from the 1920s.

On one wall was a series of sound-making panels, on another dozens of specimen bags containing tactile natural objects. There was also a den for children to climb into. A series of light/touch/visual boxes surrounding a circular display utilised many practical aids including a braille globe of the world, raised print images, and sound sensors. Blindfolds, distorting goggles, eyeshades and earmuffs allowed an appreciation of varying levels of sensory distortion. Cloaks, masks and costumes were also provided for dressing-up and could be worn around the exhibition.

The exit from this exhibition led down a temporary ramp to the gallery of social history where a smaller, dramatically lit installation of white drapes surrounded a series of sculptures entitled *Computer Transformation* by Mark Dunhill. These pieces were intended to be handled and identified while blindfolded.

Workshops throughout the course of the exhibition included "touch" sessions in which specimens were handled. These proved particularly successful with groups of blind children and children with learning difficulties. *Another Way of Seeing* attracted 3,500 people (including 1,387 school children) as against 230 visitors the previous month. The exhibition had to be extended by a week due to its popularity.

The whole project was conceived with disabled people in mind, and the gallery therefore had to reconsider its accessibility. With a positive attitude, great willingness on the part of the then curator Willy Milne and assistance from an active local access committee, much was achieved to this end. Plans were implemented to improve all signage and lighting throughout the museum for the benefit of visually impaired visitors. The temporary lift and toilet facilities were soon replaced with permanent ones, and wheelchair and chairlifts were installed with funding assistance from ADAPT (see page 39) and the Carnegie (UK) Trust.

Tate Gallery, Liverpool

In 1989, the Tate, Liverpool, hosted a Royal National Institute for the Blind (RNIB) seminar entitled "Art Education and Visual Impairment". In response to this, and in a bid to attract more visually impaired visitors to the gallery, *New Light on Sculpture* was devised.

The exhibition, which ran between December 1990 and February 1991, was organised by curator Lewis Biggs and head of education Toby Jackson, with assistance from art and visual impairment consultant William Kirby. Additional help was given by Richard Latto from the Department of Psychology at Liverpool University; the Royal National College for the Blind, Hereford and the RNIB; and sponsorship was provided by Barclays Bank plc and Concord Lighting.

Using works from its own sculpture collection, among them pieces by Henry Moore and Barbara Hepworth, and complemented by works by contemporary artists such as Richard Deacon and Tony Cragg, an exhibition was devised of contrasting shape, surface and scale. Geared to a visually impaired *and* sighted audience, *New Light on Sculpture* emphasised a new way of looking which involved interpretation through the interactive processes of touch, smell, hearing and memory, and for those with some residual vision, through visual means. By using experimental lighting techniques the exhibition high-lighted, low-lighted and enhanced the artworks for greater appreciation.

Linear Construction (1970–71), by Naum Gabo, was suspended within a dark alcove where it rotated slowly. A halo effect was created using spotlights to pick out the edges of its delicate form, creating the illusion of it floating in mid-air. This was contrasted by neighbouring *Atom Piece*

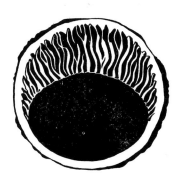

Linear Construction, by Naum Gabo, was suspended within a dark alcove where it rotated slowly. A halo effect was created using spotlights to pick out the edges of its delicate form, creating the illusion of it floating in mid-air.

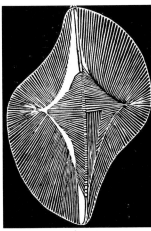

Sally Cutler's catalogue illustration of *Tondo* by Stephen Cox

Tondo: *We Must Always Turn South* (1981) by Stephen Cox. Photograph: Christian Smith, LBIPP

Sally Cutler's catalogue illustration of *Linear Construction* (1970–71) by Naum Gabo

(1964), a large, unrelenting bronze sculpture by
Henry Moore. Barbara Hepworth's *Menhirs* (1964)
in black slate were contrasted against a light
background, giving movement through slits of
light. Their cold, silken surface contrasted with the
warmth of touch and colour provided by Stephen
Cox's wall-mounted, sun-like *Tondo: We Must
Always Turn South* (1981).

Kiss and Tell (1989), by Richard Deacon,
contains many contradictions. Its rough surface of
wood and metal daubed with glue and punctured
by dozens of staples belies its smooth underbelly.
The hard exterior could also be beaten by the
visitor, producing opposing echoes and thuds,
clues to the structure's mysterious interior.

Right: *Large Object* (1959) by
Hubert Dalwood. Photograph:
Christian Smith LBIPP

Sally Cutler's catalogue illustration
of *Large Object* by Hubert Dalwood

In addition to the sculptural pieces were two
installations, one of which could be walked
around. Ron Haseldon's *Shelf Life* (1990) provided
smell, heat and an individual kind of light. Slabs of
perfumed wax had been placed in random rows
upon shelves. Fluorescent lamps set the wax
aglow, melting it and changing its form over the
duration of the exhibition. Andrew Sabin's fairy-
tale forest, *Untitled* (1990), used a camouflage skin
of PVC and ceramic over a fibreglass and steel
frame to re-create the memory of a recurring
childhood dream. The "forest" could be entered,
evoking a stronger mental rather than actual
visualisation.

Since how much we are able to see depends

DET trainer Rossita Green feeling dust from Ayers Rock,
during the Michael Andrews exhibition

physically on the intensity, quality and direction of
the light source, the gallery's main lighting was
turned off and replaced by reduced, subtle lighting.
New Light on Sculpture used a variety of light
sources, positioning and backgrounds to different
effect, all with the aim of maximising and
enhancing the visually impaired visitor's experience
and aesthetic appreciation. A catalogue was
produced in large print, braille and on audio tape,
the former with bold line illustrations which
corresponded to wall-mounted labels (see page
18). In addition, an audio guide and tactile map
were provided to aid orientation.

With only 16 exhibits, *New Light on Sculpture*
was not over-demanding or exhausting, but
allowed time for thorough exploration, and space
in which to experience the physicality of the
sculptural forms, to sense their presence and
develop an awareness of their scale and meaning.
The exhibition provided a shared viewing point for
all who attended.

Whitechapel Art Gallery, London

The Whitechapel Art Gallery in the East End of London presents work by prestigious British and international artists, local artists and community groups. Foyer space is regularly given over to work produced in conjunction with the community education department, whose principle is to involve disabled people through offering workshops tailored to individual needs.

The Whitechapel organises discussions, talks and tours during every exhibition and has run many popular "touch" workshops in the past. From regular contact and consultation with blind and visually impaired visitors and artists, community education organiser Lucy Dawe Lane began looking at the possibility of moving beyond the "touch" experience to exploring two-dimensional work through concepts rather than contact.

Ideas for workshops using a variety of methods and stimuli to create a "parallel" experience to the visual approach emerged. For the Michael Andrews show, a group of nine people with visual impairments, among them artists at various stages of their career, some with partners, listened to readings from Bruce Chatwin's book *Songlines*, together with a sound track of Aboriginal music used by Andrews, and these prompted discussion of the artist's *Ayers Rock* landscape painting series. Discussion centred around memories of places, Australia, and colour vision.

With all workshops at the gallery, a "way in" to the work is devised in collaboration with the artists leading the workshop, disabled people and experienced workers in the field of arts and disability.

A workshop involving a combination of touch and text readings was held during the *Seven Obsessions* installation (August–September 1990). The starting point was a tour of the gallery to explore the artists' use of space, time and physical materials in the making of site-specific sculpture. Melanie Counsell's work was experienced through entering the space she had created, seating participants either side of her gauze screen, and discussing it in relation to the architecture of the gallery, its symmetry with the entrance and supporting pillars. Passages were read from Daniel Defoe's *Journal of a Plague Year* which Counsell had chosen to accompany her work. Exploring the gauze, participants discovered lumps of grease she had syringed into it, each squeezed and rubbed it into their fingers and smelt them. Its relation to oil paint was considered. Everyone was then given a square of newspaper to rub the grease into, and discussed how Counsell had used these two materials in the second part of her piece to create a slowly seeping change over the course of the exhibition.

Tim Head's work of black bar-code stripes from floor to ceiling on walls painted in lurid yellow, mauve, pink and blue was visible to a large number of the group. While Chris Burden's *Medusa's Head*, a large suspended globe encrusted with railway tracks, had a very physical presence. Being able to feel it in part and encircle its girth as a group was, as Lucy Dawe Lane said, "Almost a model of how the group helped each other piece together a vision of the whole show."

"There is no logical reason why visually impaired visitors should only be interested in sculpture, or that their sense of touch is the only aesthetic 'domain' of any value to them."
Lucy Dawe Lane

Group discussion of the *Ayers Rock* series by Michael Andrews

'entitled' to know

Disabled people are a potentially large part of the market for the arts, yet lack of accurate and accessible information remains a powerful deterrent for them.

Sighted people gain as much as 95 per cent of their sensory experience through their eyes. Bearing this in mind, you begin to comprehend how much information (in the form of books, catalogues, labels, notices, paintings) becomes inaccessible to visually impaired people.

Publicity is a vital element of any organisation's work, the tool by which it creates a public image. However, disabled people are frequently excluded from this. It is estimated that 1.6 million people in this country are unable to read regular news print,[1] while other sources[2] suggest the figure could be even higher, with 15,000 people totally blind and 1,700,000 with severe or appreciable sight impairment. Of these, about 4 per cent read braille.

Yet many organisations do not produce information in any alternative format, be it braille, tape cassette or large print. In 1984, the Royal National Institute for the Blind (RNIB), in co-operation with the Museums Association (MA), published a questionnaire on museum facilities for visually impaired visitors. Of the 1,400 MA members who returned them only 2.5 per cent provided braille guides; 4.5 per cent cassette guides; 3.9 per cent large-print guides; 1 per cent braille labels; and 9.9 per cent large-print labels.

Disabled people are a potentially large part of the market for the arts, yet lack of accurate and accessible information remains a powerful deterrent for them. Where facilities do exist they are often not advertised or targeted through appropriate channels, such as the specialist press, or radio and television information networks like Oracle's *Earshot* and Ceefax's *No Need to Shout*.

Access to information is not just a matter of choice on the part of service providers, but a matter of civil rights for those people denied choice, opportunity and involvement.

The application of available computer technology has not yet been widely explored in this country in relation to museums and galleries. The

[1] Office of Population Censuses and Surveys
[2] RNIB sources

Blind artist Carolyn James using a thermoform of Caravaggio's
micro gallery in the Sainsbury Wing of London's National Gallery holds catalogued information on the collection which can be accessed via a touch-screen facility requiring no keyboard skills. Systems like this could be developed (as they have been in places like the Cité des Sciences et de l'Industrie, Paris, where computers are used to decode information by vocal synthesis and braille), to provide large-print display or "information at your fingertips".

Greenwich Citizens Gallery

For the gallery's *It Makes Sense* exhibition, 1989 (see page 9), large-print and braille invitations, designed and printed by Pia, Cardiff, were packed

denied and visually impaired visitors. These three-minute tapes run continually, providing information and historical anecdotes, and creating atmosphere as people pass through the exhibition space.

The Living Paintings Trust

The trust produces and distributes "albums" which enable blind and visually impaired people to enjoy some 40 major paintings. The albums contain raised plastic relief representations of paintings called thermoforms. These are accompanied by instructions in braille and large print to aid exploration of the works by touch. Audio cassettes provide information about the artist, style and period, and give descriptions of the paintings. Colour reproductions are also included to enable visually impaired and sighted people to discover the paintings together.

The trust is a non-profit-making charity and its founders, who include both sighted and visually impaired people, are widely experienced in the creative arts. In May 1989, it won a National Art Collections award for outstanding contribution to the visual arts. The trust has established a free library service enabling people to use albums at home, and extra copies of thermoforms can be provided for group work. Classes to help people benefit fully from using thermoform have been set up with the aid of social services, blind people's societies and volunteers. The trust has also initiated a project of art education for blind and visually impaired children aged 3–16, involving three mainstream schools in north Yorkshire.

The National and Tate Galleries in London, the Burrell Collection in Glasgow, and Kettle's Yard at the University of Cambridge, are galleries which regularly use the thermoform system and with whom the trust is working to compile albums relating to their own collections. The albums not only make art accessible to totally blind people, but heighten the perception of those with residual vision.

in boxes of tissue and doused with perfume, producing a faint aroma when they arrived through the letterbox. It was the first time an art venue had used combined print and braille design and, given the low cost, it could be repeated for future exhibitions. This pioneering idea was mentioned on *In Touch,* the Radio 4 programme for visually impaired people.

Tullie House, Carlisle City Museum and Art Gallery

Audio labels for museum displays at Tullie House (see page 43) benefit everyone, in particular print-

a catalogue of success

A number of imaginative exhibition catalogues have been produced for multi-sensory and "touch" shows where access has been a high priority. Creating such catalogues can present designers with a creative challenge, but the results often prove successful on an aesthetic as well as a practical level. More importantly, consideration of disabled people's needs should be made for all exhibition catalogues, not only those targeted at disabled people.

New Light on Sculpture

For its *New Light on Sculpture* exhibition 1990–91 (see page 13), the Tate Gallery, Liverpool, produced a large-print catalogue with black and white lino-cut illustrations by Sally Cutler, which could be seen by many visually impaired readers. These illustrations were repeated alongside their respective sculptures to assist identification. Catalogue text was also translated into braille and onto audio tape.

Revelation for the Hands

The catalogue which accompanied *Revelation for the Hands* – an exhibition of "sculpture to touch" held at Leeds City Art Gallery and the University of Warwick Art Centre in 1987 – was the first of its kind in this country and set a new precedent. Devised by Adam White, curator at the Leeds City Art Gallery, it incorporated large-print descriptions of artworks, with details of dimensions and materials, to aid touch interpretation, and bold illustrations all clearly numbered to correspond to the text. The catalogue was also produced in braille and tape format. Audio guides and relief maps representing the layout of the exhibition were also available.

Art by Disabled People

Stoke City Museum and Art Gallery's *Art by Disabled People* exhibition, 1989 (see page 41), had an accompanying catalogue written by Jim Shea, senior assistant keeper, fine art/information. The catalogue was informative and educational, explaining disability issues, politics and disability culture clearly and simply. It defined the social model of disability, explaining why the medical model is no longer appropriate.

Virtual Realities

The large-format catalogue produced for The Scottish Arts Council's Travelling Gallery summer exhibition *Virtual Realities* (see page 62), was designed to give braille equal weight to the printed text and to make it an integral part of the publication. Text was printed large-scale and had transparent braille overlays. Images were produced in duotone with high tonal contrasts. It was designed and printed with HMSO Scotland at a cost of £6,500 for a print run of 1,000.

BP re-Vision

For Greenwich Citizens Gallery's *BP re-Vision* exhibition, 1992 (see page 9), a spiral-bound, illustrated catalogue incorporated acetate sheets of braille text overlaying very large - print text. It worked on both practical and aesthetic/design levels.

Horse and Rider. Bold black and white catalogue illustrations correspond with those on wall-mounted labels alongside each sculpture to ease identification of exhibits in the British Museum's Wolfson Gallery.

2 a lot to shout about

in the picture

"We are not portrayed anywhere except as brave sufferers in the media or upon charities' posters. We are not supposed to have rights and choices, only pity and charity. Nowhere is there a clear understanding or support of the issues and problems affecting disabled people's lives. We are portrayed as slaves to our medical conditions, forever dependent, whilst the social disability, that which society puts on us, is ignored or patronised."

David Hevey

Representation of disabled people by charities' advertising tends to use negative stereotypes for the manipulation of the emotions, evocation of guilt and stirring of consciences of non-disabled people, which can only be salved by them dipping into their pockets to fill charities' begging bowls. Billboard advertising, often comprising monochromatic photo images, reinforces the misconceptions held by the non-disabled about disabled people, and is thus socially divisive.

Significant change is dependent upon disabled people taking control of their lives, representation and images.

Camerawork, London

Camerawork, formerly the Halfmoon Photography Workshop, has been based in the East End of London since 1975. It specialises in contemporary photography and its name is wholly appropriate since it is concerned as much with the process as with the end product, having both darkroom and finishing space, and a gallery for exhibiting work.

A programme of exhibitions, workshops, outreach work, courses, events and darkroom hire is undertaken by Camerawork's eight staff, and the education programme plays a central role within these. Until 1985, *Camerawork Magazine* was produced on the premises which, along with touring exhibitions such as *No Access* and *Visions of the Blind*, broke new ground in photography and disability.

The work the organisation undertakes is proactive and diverse, but entirely issue-based,

often concerning current national and international events and debates. Themes are initiated both internally and externally, and projects are often the result of collaboration with other organisations. With the Photo Co-Op, London (now Photofusion), Camerawork produced the exhibition *Bodies of Experience: Stories about Living with HIV,* told through images and narrative.

Camerawork has a long tradition of consultation with disabled people and they form a significant part of its steering committee. Hence the exhibition programme places much emphasis on disability issues. In 1987, Camerawork hosted the conference "Representing Disability in Photography", looking at charities' control of representation. An exhibition entitled *A Sense of Self* (July–August 1988), emerged from the conference and out of a growing realisation that disabled people had an inadequate sense of self-awareness and potential.

Claire & Geraldine in Love (Again) by David Hevey

This exhibition used colour images in contrast to the black-and-white social documentary photography traditionally used when portraying disabled people. Dealing with disabled people taking control of their own representation, Camerawork recognised that the exhibition would provoke mixed response, but by taking risks it succeeded in promoting open debate on the issues involved and thus raised public awareness.

The aim of *A Sense of Self* was to provide the opportunity for disabled people to explore the

Left: *Shoot-up Hill Office Door Handle*
Right: *Painting Round the Edge of Dad's Front Door* and *David Bowie's Door.* All by Johnnie and Maggie Gathercole from *Beyond the Barriers*

processes of self-discovery and to experiment further with photography. They could then start to match self-awareness to photographic image, demonstrating their creativity and individuality.

The exhibition was important because the control was in the hands of disabled people and non-disabled people were not the facilitators. It featured 60 works reflecting the different perspectives of disabled artists Caroll Pinkham, Imogen Young and David Hevey, and the groups they worked with.

A Sense of Self challenged the traditional relationship of the photographer and the sitter, and the non-disabled value judgements which had characterised images of disabled people for so long and with which disabled people were extremely dissatisfied. The exhibition looked at new sources of images. Thus, one of the alternatives to traditional stereotyping was the work of David Hevey, who tries to convey a sense of power in his subjects, namely disabled people, through "the assertive gaze".

His photograph of Derek from Effra Trust, an ex-offenders' hostel for people with epilepsy, shows a man in an institutional setting where nothing appears to belong to him. Hevey alters the viewer's impression of the sitter by addressing the subject directly. Through the closeness and height of the photographer to the sitter, he also implies that the two are in conversation, thereby creating a sense of intimacy and understanding.

A Sense of Self, staged in conjunction with conferences, workshops and talks which explored disability issues, toured to 13 venues around the UK, not just to galleries but to non-art venues such as community centres and colleges of higher education.

Some of the emergent issues were the types of representation in charities' advertising – the "tragic" medical model, the begging victim "cap-in-hand". Other issues such as personal relationships were touched upon, and these gave rise to a follow-on exhibition around the subject of sexuality and relationships, *Beyond the Barriers*.

Beyond the Barriers questioned how much of

a sense of self-image is affected by overriding stereotypes and by images of a culture which itself places a high value on physical beauty and wholeness and seeks to deny difference. It explored how disabled people are often denied sexuality, how sexuality manifests itself in disabled people and how it is perceived and received by others. This provoked many questions. Disabled people expend much energy in making non-disabled people feel comfortable around them. Should they try to please others at the expense of themselves and should they hide their true feelings?

Work was commissioned from David Hevey, Mary Duffy (see page 24) and Johnnie and Maggie Gathercole. Elspeth Morrison, the editor of *Disability Arts in London* (see page 29) and Ruth Bailey of *London Disability Arts Forum* (see page 30) acted as advisers during the project which was funded by the Arts Council, Greater London Arts (now London Arts Board), the London Boroughs Grants Scheme and CETA (photographic) Labs.

Above: *Andrew Miah* by David Hevey from *Beyond the Barriers.* "There are a lot of things that have formed me. The hostel where I live, my colour, my sexuality and having epilepsy. It takes you a long time to sort all this out, but even when things have been at their most difficult I have kept my Friday shift at the South Africa House picket in London. For me, the fight against racism is as important as sexuality and as important as disability." Andrew Miah

The work by Johnnie Gathercole and his sister and collaborator Maggie, was important in that it dealt with hidden or non-visible disability making *Beyond the Barriers* the first mainstream touring exhibition to address such issues.

David Hevey

David Hevey is an experienced disabled photographer. His numerous freelance commissions on disability have included photography for exhibition and promotion, publication and television. "While my photographic work is primarily a tool of the disability movement, I have also worked very much at the interface between our movement and its effects on other groups," says Hevey.

Work has been commissioned from a wide range of organisations, from independent photographic galleries, such as Camerawork, through to the Labour and trades union movement, where he has used photography as a propagandist tool, rather than as a tool of personal expression.

Striking Poses, one of Camerawork's touring exhibitions, was produced by Hevey in collaboration with the GRAEAE Theatre Company.

Working over a period of six weeks in two London schools, Hevey and the GRAEAE Theatre in Education team combined photography with drama. Through the use of large-format Polaroid cameras, backdrops and studio lighting, costume and role play, they produced a theatrical and visually exciting exhibition which toured nationwide. Talks, workshops and discussions accompanied the exhibition and looked at ways of facilitating photographic production by disabled people and access to photography education and the arts.

Through his work for various organisations which often work in visual isolation of each other, Hevey gradually saw the need for one major initiative to draw together common elements and themes. Thus the idea of *Creatures* evolved.

The Creatures Time Forgot. Photography and Disability Imagery by Hevey encompasses a publication (Routledge, 1992), an education pack introducing the issues and politics of disability, a series of disability imagery-awareness training days, talks and conferences — all produced in conjunction with the Arts Council and Camerawork — a poster campaign, and a touring photographic exhibition (organised by Camerawork). The overall cost of the project (over £70,000) was met by the Rowntree Foundation, the Arts Council, London Arts Board and Camerawork, with additional assistance from Hoskins plc .

Right: *Gerry McGrath: The Shifting Sands of HIV*. Part one of four from *The Creatures Time Forgot* (1992) by David Hevey. The blurring is deliberate, simulating the circulation of HIV in the human body. The rough borders symbolise society's fragile attempts to contain the virus.

In order to redress the negative portrayal of disabled people in charities' advertising and as a direct attack on the "pornography of pity", Hevey presents us with positive and empowering imagery. He also addresses the problem of getting the work seen by as wide an audience as possible using the formats detailed above, with the overall aim of creating a powerful resource of disability imagery that is widely available and accessible in terms of distribution and cost.

One of the central debates around disability representation which Hevey confronts is that of black-and-white versus colour photography; black and white being the metaphor for welfarism and the victim, while colour represents the "Brave New World". Hevey also explores secondary issues of representation and the need for propaganda, for "leaving our mark without continually having to be physically present", which consolidates the central issues of access and power. Questions such as: What is positive imagery? What methods go into it? How does it work? and Who controls it? are all considered.

The exhibition opened at Camerawork on 6 April 1992. In four parts, all exploring particular aspects of the process of disability representation, it comprised *The Sites of Disablement,* a series of three-foot-square portraits relating to work-place disability, and in particular, building sites; *The Shifting Sands of HIV*, produced with HIV activist Gerry McGrath about living with HIV, and the issue of death expectancy which society imposes on people impaired by HIV; *Liberty, Equality, Disability – Images of a Movement*, made up of seven large colour posters exploring issues of access, self-worth, education, employment and sexuality through imagery and text; and *In the Charity Camp*, a spoof on charities' advertising, which included images entitled *Thank You for Putting Us in Colour* and *Cap in Hand*.

Hevey has spent much time committing his theory to pen in addition to photographic image. He believes we need to define what we mean by positive and negative images and that we must now go beyond these to ask the central question: how do we show oppression without showing victims?

For Hevey, oppressive disability imagery is contained within what he calls "the tragedy principle". From Richard III to James Bond villains, the principle has meant that disability has been portrayed as bodily impairment, as a social or personal flaw. Hevey argues that it is this principle which we need to break. The *Creatures* training pack, entitled *Beyond the Tragedy Principle* and funded by the Joseph Rowntree Foundation, aims to bring about this breakage and transformation.

Valley and Vale

Valley and Vale are community arts workers who run workshops and courses in video, photography, dance, drama and music throughout the Ogwr and Vale of Glamorgan districts of south Wales. Established in 1981, with the aim of encouraging participation by local people in the development of their communities through the arts, they work collectively with groups traditionally disenfranchised from effective means of communication.

Past projects have included a photographic exhibition highlighting access to public buildings for wheelchair users in the Bridgend area, and a video, *Disability/Capability* (1985), which explored society's attitudes to disability.

Self Portrait was an exhibition of work by people with learning difficulties created during 1988. It was the result of a photography project organised by Valley and Vale in Llanfrechfa Grange near Cwmbran, a residential hospital, where residents made and selected images of themselves.

For *Self Portrait,* workshops were devoted to developing the skills necessary to make choices such as body position and facial expression, what to wear, where the portrait should be shot and what objects to include within the frame. Using cable-release the group members were able to become both photographers and subjects at once. A darkroom facility was established at the hospital enabling them to develop and print their own photographs. Sixty photographs became an exhibition which represented a strong statement about the abilities of people who are classified as "mentally handicapped".

The exhibition was first shown at the hospital. Chapter Art Centre, Cardiff then hosted it for one month in spring 1989. It was also set to travel to the Netherlands as part of a festival of work by artists throughout Wales. However, in the week it was due to leave, two consultants at the hospital decided the photographs could not be shown as they believed the exhibition did not represent "a positive image" of people with learning difficulties.

This judgement took little account of the fact that the photographs were taken and developed by the residents themselves, who in most cases selected them as their favourite images. In preventing the exhibition from being shown, the hospital authorities effectively said they did not believe the residents were capable of making their own choices on such issues.

The first step in attempting to change society's misrepresentations of people with learning difficulties must be to encourage people who have been marginalised in this way to speak for themselves, to create their own images. If these images are sometimes uncomfortable, perhaps we need to question whether what is conventionally accepted as a positive image is often an assimilation of the subject into the "normal" world.

Projects like *Self Portrait* are a small step in the direction of empowering and enabling people to gain more control over the course of their own lives and to begin to define who they are and what they feel. These definitions become influential and they are seen widely. A touring exhibition can change attitudes. To this day the exhibition remains banned.

Mary Duffy

Mary Duffy lives in Bray, Co. Wicklow, Northern Ireland, and attended the National College of Art and Design, Dublin, where she studied photography in her final year. She now uses this training to explore body image. Duffy feels she is surrounded by images of women that are far removed from her own reality. Her work represents her response to this, and her experience and feelings as a disabled woman.

Prejudice & Pride by Mary Duffy is part of a series of six works (actual size 60" x 30") dealing with disability and personal relationships, commissioned by Camerawork, London.

somebody's daughter
CHILD

i am your daughter
i was born in your double bed
you thought i was half bird
that i had wings

afterwards you thought
god had chosen you specially for me,
and you were going to love me so much
it wouldn't make any difference

they blamed it on sputnik and the russians and gave me
artificial arms when i was eight months old
they came out of the airing cupboard every morning
to help me develop a body image that included arms
while we all waited for technology to catch up.

i am to be discouraged from using my feet,
and 'bionic' limbs arrive when i am five years old
they are big heavy hooks
powered by gas cylinders
and you send them back after two weeks

with them go all attempts
to make my body conform

my own
WOMAN

i am growing up,
and you think i will never go away,
that i will always live with you
be washed and dressed by you
the perfect offspring who never leaves the nest

you teach me to be independent,
to be strong,
to have my own opinions,
to earn my own living
neither of us knows
that one day i will dress and wash myself
and live independently

but i haven't been programmed or conditioned
to be anybody's wife,
lover,
or mother,
you didn't teach me to serve anybody,
to wash or peel potatoes,

you appreciate my intelligence,
creativity, wit, sharpness
and humour
you call me máire cock
by refusing to inoculate me against rubella,
you ignore my sexuality

sisters
DEPENDENCE

until i was seventeen
i depended on you
to bring me to the toilet
every day of my life.
it gave you power
power to care,
control,
manipulate,
hurt,
and humiliate
one hot summer's day i pissed in the school yard
because you would not bring me to the toilet
i felt terrible despair
and anger,
as the steam rose from my urine
trickling towards the gutter.
today i do not understand,
why i did not break the cycle
and simply ask someone else to help me

sisters
LOVE

you accused me of always letting you down
just when you needed me most,
and i made you smile and forget your anger
by crooning
"you always hurt the one you love,
the one you shouldn't hurt at all"

for me, loving you is unconditional
and it shouldn't hurt
you're my oldest friend, my nearest and dearest,
my childhood, adulthood, past and present
you are funny,
warm and indomitable

for me loving you is about letting go
the fear of being hurt,
vulnerable and powerless
it is about defining my own space and saying no
it is about forgiveness
and about letting go the feeling
of being responsible for your happiness

out of the dark

Photography is a useful and effective means by which disabled people can represent themselves, countering negative, stereotypical portrayals of themselves by others. A small number of darkrooms around the country have been adapted or purpose-built for use by disabled people. Many have developed innovative approaches to photography through workshops and long-term projects where participants find the creative means to express their experience of disability.

Community and Recreational Arts in Barnet (CRAB)

CRAB is an umbrella organisation which comprises two dance groups, Happy Go Lucky and Oddsox, and London's first fully accessible darkroom and photographic studio, Community Focus. Its work is supported by the London Arts Board, the London Borough Grants Scheme, the London Borough of Barnet, trusts, private companies and donations.

Community Focus is based at Tedder Studio, a previously under-used community building on the Grahame Park Estate in Hendon. In 1987, Barnet Council offered these premises, once a target for vandalism, to CRAB, which converted them into a fully wheelchair-accessible photography arts centre. The centre is respected by local people for its positive effect on the community.

Community Focus has worked primarily with disabled people since 1978, but it welcomes the input of non-disabled people who wish to share in the activities. However, the overall aim is to initiate and encourage demand for participatory workshops by individuals and groups traditionally excluded from the arts.

With level access throughout, and equipment and facilities which have been adapted to overcome technical problems encountered by disabled people, it provides a unique London-wide facility where disabled people can learn, practise and develop their photography and work towards full control of the organisation.

Darkroom facilities at the centre include an adjustable height enlarger with computerised controls, two manual enlargers, benches and sinks with lever taps, all at wheelchair-accessible heights. Enlarger timers on movable brackets have large buttons and digits, which are particularly suitable for visually impaired users, and all lighting is suspended from ceiling rails to avoid causing obstruction. Community Focus also has a mobile darkroom which can be erected in or out of doors, allowing for a programme of outreach work in schools, day centres and hospitals.

For one project, a sculptor and photographer were engaged as artists-in-residence in a local school for disabled children, with the aim of encouraging the school to go on to use the resources at the centre on a continued basis. Following a fundraising campaign in 1991, CRAB placed a mixed-media artist-in-residence in two schools in Bårnet and Brent. With input from Community Focus, children have been able to explore two- and three-dimensional art forms. Other new initiatives include the formation of a partially sighted photography group and reminiscence art group.

Residential trips are regularly arranged for members. In July 1991, Community Focus spent a week in Yorkshire where the group visited the Yorkshire Sculpture Park (see page 87) and the National Museum of Photography, Film and Television in Bradford.

Community Focus also runs the City and Guilds "Starting Photography" course which leads to certification. The course is widely advertised in several formats including tape for blind and visually impaired people, and in a variety of media, from specialist journals such as *Amateur Photographer* and *The British Journal of Photography*, to the broader disability press.

CRAB has a commitment to expand its visual arts work, prioritising work by disabled people and developing stronger links with black and Asian communities. To this end it has built an extension at the centre to increase the variety and number of workshops which support and promote the work of marginalised people.

In the past, exhibitions which have resulted from work at the centre have been held elsewhere. *First Exposure*, an exhibition which celebrated the work of local disabled people, was shown at Hendon Library during March 1990 before touring to other wheelchair-accessible venues. Former exhibitions were toured to day centres, residential homes, festivals and disability arts days all over Britain.

CRAB frequently commissions visiting artists to initiate exhibition work. One successful project, which ran in February 1991, involved black writer Linda King who worked for 10 weeks on a combined writing–photography project with Community Focus members. Three disabled women wrote pieces about their lives and illustrated them with photographic self-portraits. They visited a desktop publishing company to learn about graphic design before choosing a style for printing their written work. The exhibition, *To Put You in the Picture*, toured to local libraries and centres.

Eliminating Shadows: A Manual on Photography and Disability
(Pub., London Print Workshop)

At a time when more disabled people are involved in the practice of photography, both at professional and amateur level, *Eliminating Shadows* reflects and meets the demand for clearer, up-to-date information specifically geared to their needs.

Written and researched by Ronald and Ray Cooper, this 118-page book contains clear line drawings by Rehabilitation Engineering Movement Advisory Panels (REMAP) showing adapted equipment ranging from the basics, such as a grip for left-hand camera operation, to the sophisticated Bell Crank Shutter Release. Other diagrams demonstrate how to improve access to both equipment and space on a do-it-yourself basis using second-hand material where available.

Existing specialist organisations, such as CRAB (see page 26), the Disabled Photographers' Society and other community organisations around the country are described, giving details of what each

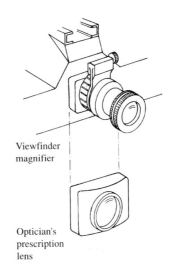

Viewfinder magnifier

Optician's prescription lens

VIEWFINDER AIDS

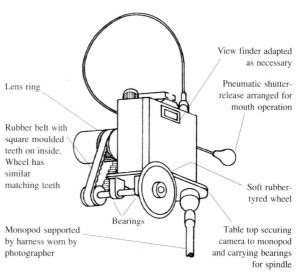

View finder adapted as necessary

Pneumatic shutter-release arranged for mouth operation

Lens ring

Rubber belt with square moulded teeth on inside. Wheel has similar matching teeth

Bearings

Monopod supported by harness worn by photographer

Soft rubber-tyred wheel

Table top securing camera to monopod and carrying bearings for spindle

CHIN OPERATED LENS ADJUSTMENT
VIEW FROM BEHIND AND BELOW CAMERA

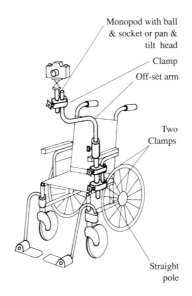

Monopod with ball & socket or pan & tilt head

Clamp

Off-set arm

Two Clamps

Straight pole

MOBILIA POLE & CLAMP SYSTEM
USED TO ATTACH CAMERA TO
WHEELCHAIR

Mobilia

has to offer and degree of accessibility.

In addition to the illustrations, there is a guide to equipment, giving detailed specifications, e.g. weight and body dimensions, and where left-handed operation is possible. Accessories such as flash cable release, waist-level viewfinders and focusing screens are discussed in terms of uses and availability. Camera supports such as tripods, straps and clamps for wheelchair users, waist-belt supports and adjustable support arms are reviewed, together with designers and suppliers, and lists are given of organisations which specialise in customised design solutions for disabled people.

For studio work at home and in community premises, the book deals with equipment, fittings and layout, offering advice on key problems such as lighting for wheelchair users. Similarly for darkrooms, whether bathrooms at home or in community darkrooms, equipment such as motorised enlargers, audible timers, film processing and loading aids are looked at, as are important safety precautions such as ventilation.

The manual considers photography for visually impaired people, aiming to counter the stereotyped ideas of what blind people can and cannot do. It examines new techniques and ways of developing latent vision.

There is a discussion on the use of the darkroom for enhancement of visual awareness, tactile representations of visual images, such as thermoforms (see page 17), and the use of personal computers to process prints.

Another section of the manual deals with arts and disability, disability culture and the language of disability. The disability arts movement is described and the main issues currently being debated are outlined. One of these is photography as an art form and as a means of self-expression and self-representation which allows disabled people to counter negative stereotypical images of themselves. Contacts and a further reading list are given.

The manual is printed in large text and its layout makes it easy to follow. The overall focus is on practical, economical ideas which will enable and encourage disabled people to practise photography independently.

Battersea Arts Centre, London

This centre has ramped access and a lift to the first floor which provides converted darkroom space for various projects aimed at disabled people. The darkroom was partially adapted in 1987 and is now being made fully accessible. It already has variable-height work benches, adequate space for wheelchair users, and such fixtures as extending taps and light cords.

In 1992, the centre ran a series of photographic courses, each consisting of six four-hour workshops, under the title "Lightworks". Targeted at adults with learning difficulties, visually impaired and other disabled people, the course sought to give participants a grounding in black-and-white, colour and infra-red photography. Workshops were run by two disabled artists, with groups of no more than 10, covering subjects such as darkroom technique and composition.

Sally O'Shea explores a Barbara Hepworth sculpture using her feet, with Rory Frances (community arts officer, YSP), Danny Ferry (Community Focus worker) and John Crowther (volunteer) at Yorkshire Sculpture Park.
Photograph: John Mason, CRAB

off the shelf

A number of national arts magazines are now giving space over to discuss access and disability issues relating to art venues and disabled people's art. In 1991 and 1992, the visual arts magazines *Artists' Newsletter, Women's Art Magazine* and *Frieze* each ran features highlighting contemporary issues affecting the lives and practice of disabled artists, with articles by disabled people. During the same period, several arts magazines by disabled people were also established. These act as a vital platform from which the profile of art by disabled people can be raised, and interest and new activity generated.

Disability Arts in London (DAIL)

DAIL is a monthly "what's on" of disability arts events taking place predominantly, but not exclusively, in London. Written for and by disabled people, it is the best available source of information on the disability arts movement. *DAIL* features previews, reviews and letters which address current issues and debates with black-and-white photographs, cartoons and a quarterly section dealing with arts developments for deaf and partially deaf people. *DAIL* also carries advertisements for equal opportunity posts in the arts and allied sectors, nationwide.

Co-ordinated by Elspeth Morrison, and produced and distributed in collaboration with Artsline (see page 51) and London Disability Arts Forum (see page 30), it is free to disabled people but costs organisations £15 per annum. It is available in print, braille and on cassette.

Disability Arts Magazine (DAM)

DAM is a quarterly magazine run by disabled people. First published in 1991, it concentrates on issues pertinent to the north of England. Past articles have included interviews with former Arts Minister Timothy Renton and profiles of artists. Disabled contributors are paid for photographs, articles, poetry and reviews.

Disability Now (DN)

DN is a monthly paper which carries a regular arts

Ballooning Over the Allotments by Maureen Golding who featured in the summer 1991 issue of DAM magazine

section. This features exhibition reviews of both disability and mainstream arts by disabled artists such as Adam Reynolds and Gioya Steinke. In the past, there have been profiles of other disabled artists, including Carolyn James and Stephen Wiltshire, and articles on hidden disability by David Hevey (see page 22) and charities' advertising.

Mailout

This is a national arts magazine focusing on community arts and under-represented areas such as disability arts and black arts. It includes examples of good practice, information on training and funding and is free on subscription through selected Regional Arts Boards.

What's Going On?

A monthly newsletter published by East Midlands Arts, *What's Going On* features an access update on arts venues in the region and current news items on access issues. It is heavily weighted toward projects and information relevant to disabled people in the arts, including festivals, events and workshops. It is produced in large-print format.

Partnerships

Produced by Artlink West Midlands, *Partnerships* highlights issues of arts and disability, arts and mental health and arts in old age.

cause for celebration

A Drop in the Ocean (detail) by Adam Reynolds

The emergence in this country of the disability arts movement, acting through a national network of disability arts forums, is helping disabled people find their own identity and culture in a mainly white male-dominated world. Its arguments are similar to those of the black arts and women's movements, where the issue is not just about joining a system but changing it. The movement fosters separatism in order to develop — through a collective voice and mobilising of strength — a power base from which to exercise rights before joining the mainstream "system".

Left with a legacy of care and cure interventions which have encouraged dependency, disabled people are now demanding the right to redefine and dictate the images and issues of disability, the right to represent themselves. As David Hevey (see page 22) says: "Representation is not just a side show of the movement, but integral to the struggle."

The resulting artwork by disabled people challenges assumptions about the monetary value and meaning of art; art as a commodity; and the "what sells defines" principle. Groups of disabled people, once voiceless, are now vocal through visual means through sign language, performance and visual art, and this articulation is bringing with it choice and control. Disability arts reflect the experience and the struggle — both the personal and political — of disabled people who have remained on the margins of society for too long.

Disability Arts and Culture Seminar

The increasing number of disability arts festivals and forums, and disability television programmes and magazines, is evidence of both a growth in momentum and funding, and of the higher profile the arts now have in the lives of disabled people. The concept of a "disability culture" is increasingly being discussed, but its significance and implications for wider cultural debate and development are as yet unclear.

In collaboration with the Open University and *Disability Arts in London* magazine (see page 29), Shape London organised a major seminar at

Willesden Green Library Centre, north-west London, in November 1991 to clarify these areas. This one-day disability arts and culture seminar aimed to review developments and address such questions as: Who controls disability arts? Who are its members and audiences? How does it contribute to the wider disability movement? and What is its relationship to the wider arts industries and mainstream cultures?

Funded by the Arts Council, the seminar was attended by 33 disabled arts practitioners from around the country. A panel of speakers included Sian Vasey (see below) on definitions of disability arts and culture, Elspeth Morrison (see page 29) and Vic Finkelstein on access to power, and David Hevey (see page 22) on strategies for change. Presentation papers from the seminar together with a summary of questions and group discussions, have been published by, and are available from, Shape London priced £5.

London Disability Arts Forum (LDAF)

Founded in 1986, LDAF was, as Sian Vasey put it, "born out of the political consciousness of disabled people and the idea of disabled people controlling the resources available, the administration of the activity and the decisions taken about what events should happen".

The first of a growing number of regional disability arts forums, it provides a platform from which the work, talent and ideas of disabled artists can be expressed and developed. LDAF facilitates discussion and awareness of disability issues, and promotes standards and procedures of good practice both for itself and for others. It co-produces *Disability Arts in London* magazine (see page 29) with Artsline (see page 51) and organises Workhouse, a cabaret club run for and by disabled people in venues all over London, which encapsulates the spirit of the disability arts movement.

In September 1991, LDAF co-ordinated a European festival bringing together disabled artists from Europe for the first time in a day of workshops, discussion, cabaret and celebration.

Held in Tottenham, north London, this "Euro-Day" included an exhibition of work by disabled artists and an unveiling of a commissioned sculpture *Shaken not Stirred* by Tony Heaton.

National Disability Arts Forum (NDAF)

NDAF was founded in 1990, with representatives from each Regional Arts Board area. Controlled by disabled people and chaired by Sian Vasey (see page 30), its original role was to channel funds from the European Community through The European Committee on Creativity by and for Disabled People (see page 58) to disability arts projects in this country. It soon became a vehicle for the development and promotion of disability arts and culture, giving the disability arts movement a power base from which to campaign.

North West Disability Arts Forum (NWDAF)

Established in February 1990, NWDAF evolved out of the work and achievements of Arts Integration Merseyside. Originally based at the Crawford Arts Centre, it has moved to a permanent base at the Centre for Arts Development Training, where it shares resources. A limited company, with charitable status pending, it employs two full-time development officers supported by a part-time administrator.

Informed, managed and staffed by disabled people, NWDAF offers advice and support to practising disabled artists and to those disabled people seeking training in a particular art form. It frequently works alongside existing arts organisations, with the purpose of influencing policy and provision relating to access issues. Working across all art forms, and in a variety of contexts, NWDAF strives to alter and improve the nature of provision and puts disability arts issues on the agenda.

The forum "operates at the heart of arts activity in the region, not on the fringe". As such, it receives mainstream arts funding through the North West Arts Board and local authorities. One of NWDAF's long-term priorities is to more actively involve disabled people from black, Asian and Chinese communities in its work.

Above: *Hanging up in Hounslow* from the *Louder Than Words* festival with Nancy Willis. **Photograph: Ted Bath, The Times**

Shape London Festivals

In the early days of the disability arts movement, festivals celebrating the work and achievements of disabled artists and performers lasted a day. By the beginning of the 1990s they had grown to a week or more in length. *Louder Than Words* lasted six weeks and took place during March and April 1992 in Hounslow.

The Hounslow Festival Committee decided to include the boroughs of Richmond and Ealing to make the festival the largest of its sort ever to be staged in London. Artists from around the country participated and events were co-ordinated at accessible venues throughout the three boroughs. These included a sign-dance performance by Theatre Venture with a cast of deaf and hearing performers, a deaf arts seminar, visual arts exhibitions, video events and workshops, and cabaret.

In 1991, the visual arts element of the festival – *Hanging up in Hounslow* – was held at the newly converted accessible Orangery gallery in Gunnersbury Park, west London. Work by disabled artists Trevor Landell (see page 92), Nancy Willis (see page 90), Lucy Jones and Adam Reynolds (see pages 4 and 29) was hung alongside work by artists from day centres. In 1992, *Way Out West*, an exhibition of works by professional disabled artists, was held at the Small Mansion Arts Centre, also at Gunnersbury Park, while the Orangery hosted *Three Into Two Goes*, a touring exhibition of two-

Marc Chagall's The Blue Violinist by Tommy Mason from Attitude

Gargoyles in the making by Adam Reynolds. Photograph: Gordon Cooper

and three-dimensional work by artists from day centres and community groups.

Coinciding with the Hounslow festival was *Go Go Go '92,* the seventh Hackney festival to be organised by Shape, at Chats Palace in east London. This featured daytime workshops in visual arts, sculpture and other art forms, and evening performances by Heart 'n' Soul, GRAEAE Theatre Company and local performance groups.

Project Ability

Based in Glasgow, Project Ability was formed in response to the International Year for the Disabled in 1981. Its overall objective is to create opportunities in the arts for socially disadvantaged people encouraging integration into the main-stream. To this end it employs professional artists with skills in the visual arts, puppetry, ceramics, music, dance and drama, and matches their experience with the needs of groups. In 1990–91, up to 800 participants a week were engaged on

projects, including collaborations with international artists. However, its main concern is to develop existing facilities in the Strathclyde region.

Funded by Strathclyde Regional Council, Glasgow District Council, the Scottish Arts Council and Greater Glasgow Health Board, Project Ability was in great demand during Glasgow's year as European City of Culture, 1990. One of its commitments was to research and produce an access guide to the city's arts venues; it also assisted Arts Special Info (see page 51) in setting up its directory and database on arts and disability.

In collaboration with the Third Eye Centre, Glasgow, Project Ability organised its first major art exhibition in 1991. *Attitude* was a show of paintings by 13 artists with learning difficulties from Glasgow and people attending Mull Day Centre on the Isle of Mull. Some of the works drew inspiration from artists such as Matisse and Chagall while others reflected the Scottish landscape and its people.

Brian Jenkins, a disabled artist and one of the

Installation shots of Sally Booth exhibition, The Key Gallery Photographs : Ian Hamilton

exhibition's selectors, believed that the project's success was due to the provision of "teaching experiences, sketching trips to develop ideas, and working on large well-prepared canvasses".

Attitude was shown at the Third Eye Centre from February to March 1991, where it was co-sponsored by 3i and Strathclyde Regional Council. It then went on to form a central part of the 1991 European Colloquium on Arts and Disability held in Dublin in May 1991. Since then it has toured to venues, including one of Northern Ireland's main contemporary art galleries — the Orchard Gallery in Derry — to Aberystwyth Arts Centre and back to Scotland.

As a result of the exhibition being seen in Dublin, Project Ability was approached by a similar Belgian-based organisation, to contribute to a two-part project called "Project 12". Two Project Ability artists attended a week-long workshop in Liège in preparation for part one of "Project 12", a touring exhibition on billboards, entitled *Art in Towns.* For the Project Ability artists it was their first time abroad.

Part two of "Project 12", the gallery exhibition, opened in Dublin in December and contained nearly 180 artworks by 58 disabled artists from Europe, including 25 selected as the UK contribution.

The Arts Connection

The Arts Connection, Portsmouth, has promoted the work of disabled artists through a number of exhibitions including *Second Glance*, which presented works by 12 artists with learning difficulties from Locksheath Day Centre. Consisting mainly of abstract drawings and paintings, *Second Glance* gave artists the opportunity to display their work in the Mountbatten Gallery, Portsmouth, and other mainstream venues in Hampshire.

More than Meets the Eye, an exhibition of work by visually impaired artists, was held at the Old Town Hall Arts Centre, Havant (see page 39) between February and March 1990. With sponsorship from the Arts Council of Great Britain and the Royal National Institute for the Blind (RNIB)

it attracted over 3,000 visitors.

A follow-up exhibition, *Insights*, was held at the Arundel Gallery, West Sussex, in March 1991. Funded by the RNIB, Arun District Council and the Southern Arts Board, the exhibition featured the work of six artists, some with visual impairment, and included paintings and sculpture "made to be touched".

The Key Gallery for the Promotion of Disabled Artists

The Key Gallery in Glasgow opened its doors in December 1991. It was the brainchild of Ian Hamilton and Mansel Griffiths, both ex-art students who also attended the Royal College for the Blind, Hereford. Prior to opening the gallery, Hamilton and Griffiths worked together as an artistic team, called Hand and Mind. The gallery was the first of its kind and aims to promote art by disabled artists while also acting as a resource to encourage contact between artists and organisations, and provide a focal point for discussion of issues concerning disabled people.

With fully accessible premises provided rent-free for a year by the Glasgow & West of Scotland Society for the Blind and financial assistance from Strathclyde Regional Council and Glasgow District Council, the gallery opened a major exhibition, set up with the help of NDAF (see page 31). The exhibition featured the work of 10 disabled artists. Since then it has had a continuous programme of mixed and solo exhibitions by established artists and newcomers. Sally Booth, who took part in both Shape *Louder than Words* festivals (see page 31), and Michael O'Hara, one of the visually impaired artists who featured in *More than Meets the Eye* (see above), Havant 1990, have exhibited here. O'Hara had a 20-year retrospective.

"The ultimate objective is that galleries of this kind will not exist in the future as it is hoped that the status and opportunities offered to disabled artists will eventually be comparable to those on offer in the mainstream," say Griffiths and Hamilton.

Deciding Whether to Jump by Sally Booth

Ice Skaters at Broadgate, Liverpool Street Station by Sally Booth. (Oil on board)

art works

Giant Fish and Jumbos **exhibition, Northern Centre for Contemporary Arts**

Access for disabled people to arts practice is often limited since artists' studios are frequently located in cheap-rent derelict warehouses which are inaccessible or unsafe. A number of accessible studios have been created in response to an arts activity or project expanding beyond its originating host organisation or impetus, and becoming user-led.

The Art Studio, Sunderland

The Art Studio is based in the east end of Sunderland. It was founded in 1986 by Artists Agency (see page 59) in response to a successful art project at Cherry Knowle Psychiatric Hospital, and its users include people recovering from mental health problems. It is a thriving project aimed at enabling people to develop creatively.

In 1989, the studio became independent, with its own management team meeting once a month to determine policy and funding strategies. This comprises representatives from the studio, area health authority, Artists Agency, social services, Arts Resource, Sunderland Arts Development Agency and Training Action and Care Together (TACT).

Partly sponsored by Sunderland Health Authority, the Studio began in small premises in Norfolk Street. The organisation has since relocated to Hind Street, a large Georgian building which has individual and shared studios, and facilities for printmaking, painting, drawing and sculpture. The Studio employs two artists-in-residence — Chris Sell (part-time), founder member of Sunderland Arts Group, and Derek Hill (full-time), an MA fine-art graduate from the Royal College of Art — who have guided the project since its inception.

There are now over 50 artists using the Studio on a regular basis, none of whom have had any arts training, and the artists-in-residence give them assistance and encouragement rather than any formal teaching. Funding from the Tyne and Wear Development Corporation in 1991 made it possible to employ a development co-ordinator to organise workshops run by the Studio artists and to develop an education programme. This post is currently funded by Wearside Training and Enterprise Centre and The John Paul Getty Jnr Charitable Trust.

Open daily, artists can come as they please. Each have their own space, and materials are provided by the Studio. Artists are encouraged to work and learn alongside each other, but the emphasis is very much on self-motivation. As one artist says: "The Studio is a haven of peace, friendship and creative industry, a place I feel part of".

The policy of the project is to reach as wide a public as possible, hence time has been spent over the past two years arranging exhibitions. The first, *Giant Fish and Jumbos,* took place in October 1990 at the Northern Centre for Contemporary Art before touring the north-east region and Oxford. This marked a turning point in the Studio's development, gaining it national as well as local press coverage together with sales and commissions. Many artists subsequently arranged their own shows and two went on to gain places on fine arts degree courses. The Art Studio was runner-up in the BBC's "It's My City" competition in 1991, which aimed to find outstanding examples of inner city initiatives. It also maintains international links, and in 1991 arranged exchange visits with artists in Poland and Spain.

The Studio is open to the public twice a week. The premises are accessible to wheelchair users and many disabled people use the Studio on a regular basis, taking part in workshops. In addition, there is a programme of events happening in and around the Studio throughout

Peter Storey working at the studio, Darlington Arts Centre. Photograph: Laurence Ward, artist-in-residence

the year including open days, open workshops, visits from groups, and visits to other studios and galleries.

In January 1991, a group of fifth-formers from Spring Well Dene School for children with emotional and behavioural problems began working with Studio artists for three hours each week. These sessions provide the opportunity for school students to make new friends, feel valued for their own creative abilities and to gain a sense of independence. Many of the children are institutionalised but through working at the Studio they are encouraged to take responsibility for themselves.

The Centre for Developmental Arts, Glasgow

The centre was developed by Project Ability (see page 32). It is a multi-purpose arts workshop and exhibition space located by Argyle Street, one of Glasgow's main thoroughfares. The centre makes possible collaborative projects with established galleries, artists' studios and theatres in the area. It also provides a central space dedicated and adapted to the needs of disabled people, becoming a focus for the promotion of their work.

Since it opened in May 1991, with financial support from British Telecom, the centre has been in constant use for ceramics, painting and movement workshops, bringing people together from across the city and building on work started as part of Project Ability's outreach programme, thus enabling participants to develop their talents further.

The centre houses a fully equipped ceramics workshop where Project Ability artists can create site-specific work for a variety of community settings. Other organisations and artists have access to the kilns and firing space for their own community projects, and the space is also open to the general public through evening classes, thus making the centre an integrated arts resource.

Gallery space for exhibitions has already involved a varied programme including a postgraduate art show. Staff from day centres and community organisations are encouraged to bring groups to visit exhibitions and to discuss the work.

A growing number of Project Ability participants now visit the centre independently and, with increased confidence, are beginning to visit other galleries and museums in the city. Thus one of Project Ability's overall objectives is being realised – that of ensuring the arts experience is not limited or contained within the walls of the centre – but is seen within a wider community context.

The Creative Arts Department, The National Star Centre, Cheltenham

The department offers disabled students the opportunity to study the arts in a professional working environment (see page 75) and was designed in consultation with students. It comprises an accessible design and photographic studio, darkroom, 3D sculpture workshop, theatre and theatre studios. Opened in 1991, working areas have height-adjustable workstations using the latest equipment and technology which allow students maximum independence and self-esteem while studying a range of subjects including painting, drawing, photography, graphics, printmaking, textiles, ceramics, jewellery and sculpture.

Darlington Arts Centre, County Durham

In 1986, an innovative "care in the community" project was established by Artists Agency (see page 59) at Darlington Arts Centre to enable former residents of Aycliffe Hospital, Co. Durham, to continue their creative activities once they had moved out into the community. At the centre they work alongside others with learning difficulties from local day centres, training and resource centres, and with a resident artist and musician. Studio workshops are held three times a week at the arts centre, and being based here provides the opportunity to meet other artists and to see the regular programme of exhibitions. Their own work is frequently shown here as well as at other public venues.

All participants of the workshops fill in self-referral forms following a pre-visit trial, thus ensuring attendance remains a matter of individual choice.

"People with learning difficulties do not have the kind of freedom that most of us take for granted. The inability to voice articulate ideas or needs in written or spoken language constitutes a major curtailment of freedom for the individual who is virtually excluded from participation in mainstream society. Art-making provides one outlet for the expression and communication of thoughts and feelings."
Annalisa Smith, former artist-in-residence, Darlington Arts Centre

Peter Naisbett at the studio, Darlington Arts Centre. Photograph: Laurence Ward, artist-in-residence

The gallery at Project Ability's Centre for Developmental Art, with Barry Fielding paintings in background. Photograph: Brian Jenkins

Right: The mosaic *Head for the Hills* sited in Manchester Royal Infirmary's Reception involved over 100 people and was the culmination of trips around the Manchester area. Photograph: Sameena Hussein, Mike Cogley & Tommy Moore, SNAPS

START, Manchester

START is an arts centre and studio whose members are recovering from mental illness. It is a component of the High Elms Community Mental Health Resource of the Manchester Central Hospitals and Community Care (NHS) Trust, and is funded accordingly. Additional funding is received from the North West Arts Board, the Gulbenkian Foundation, the Carnegie (UK) Trust and Manchester City Council.

START has over 60 members, aged between 18 and 85, four full-time and three part-time staff, plus a roster of associate artists and volunteers. College and nursing students and school pupils regularly undertake placements at START.

START offers its members the opportunity to work alongside practising artists and craftspeople to acquire arts skills; they can also participate in planning and organising START's activities and serve on the executive committee. Members learn how to organise exhibitions and market their own work. The day-to-day activities of the studio are recorded by SNAPS, START's photographic project.

Work by studio members, ranging from painting and photography to ceramics and sculpture, has been exhibited in local libraries, hospitals and city art galleries. One commission included a series of large mosaics for a restaurant at Manchester Royal Infirmary.

Another START hospital-based project was the construction of a 16-foot-high timber and mosaic column on the theme of water. Sited at the Devonshire Royal Hospital in Buxton, Derbyshire, the project involved nine START members, SNAPS (working with a local group of disabled people) and over 100 patients, staff and local people.

START also works with the public via workshops and organises outings to the local countryside, art galleries and artists' studios.

In 1989, START won joint first prize in the visual arts category of the BBC TV "It's My City" competition to find examples of outstanding inner city initiatives.

3 building matters

smoothing the way

Push button door release.
Photograph: Ian Wolfenden

Right: Ian Hamilton Finlay ramp
with Wave Rock drum.
Photograph: Ian Wolfenden

Access is more than physical, it is a philosophy. As such it goes beyond practicalities to principles. Widening access relies on individuals themselves being accessible to change in order to influence and improve our built environment for the benefit of all.

Since the International Year of the Disabled in 1981, we have seen a gradual increase in

improvement schemes, particularly the installation of ramps, adapted toilet facilities and lifts. But we need to move beyond the ramp.

The new Building Regulations 1991, Part M, on provision and facilities for disabled people, has been extended to include provision for people with sensory, visual and hearing impairments. The regulations should bring about more comprehensive improvements and a greater awareness of the needs of all disabled people.

Part M also outlines the problems likely to be encountered by disabled people if care is not given to design detail. This marks a shift in awareness and approach to access issues, as did the change in terminology from "the disabled" (suggestive of a homogenous "problem" group) to "disabled people" in recognition of the individual with individual needs.

In this country, museums and art galleries are often housed in inaccessible period buildings, many of which have conservation constraints. However, practical and economic access solutions can usually be found. Wheelchair stairlifts can provide access to areas such as small galleries, and platform lifts can be installed instead of ramps to give access to different levels within a storey where space is limited. Grants for adaptations are becoming more

widely available, and specialist organisations employing qualified disabled access advisers can offer feasibility studies and tailor-made design solutions.

It is frequently the case that access improvements are made not as a result of policy decision, but in response to a rise in demand and awareness, often through exhibitions which have attracted or been targeted at disabled people, or through a disabled employee or trainee being present within an organisation. However, more stringent policies backed by legislation will need to be enforced if significant changes throughout the arts sector are to materialise.

The Harris Museum, Preston

The Harris is a magnificent Neo-Classical building situated in Preston's market square. It houses collections of 19th- and 20th-century painting, sculpture, decorative art and local history, in addition to temporary exhibitions of contemporary art.

As part of a rolling programme of alterations and repairs to the Grade 1 listed building funded by the Central Lancashire Development Corporation and City Council, Scottish poet and artist Ian Hamilton Finlay was commissioned by the Harris to provide a creative solution to a design problem surrounding the improvement of access to the museum entrance. The Harris has side entrances rather than central steps and there is insufficient linear space for a long ramp.

Working collaboratively with sculptors, carvers and painters, as well as architects, Finlay came up with the solution: a ramp of gentle gradient, wrapped around a circular stone drum on each side of the doorway, rising from street level under the portico where steps are also incorporated. Here plinths provide seating areas and render the entrance intimate and welcoming.

Integral to the fabric of the original building are Classical inscriptions, friezes and statues, and these are reflected throughout Finlay's design. To him, words are as important for their visual imagery as for their literary one. His "Wave Rock" poem carved on the drums provides an analogy for the dramatic interaction between the forces of nature — the Wave, and human intervention – the Rock — perhaps representing the museum.

The entrance area also has cartographer's signs inscribed on its glass doors, grilles around its steps and ramps, and a frieze poem entitled "How blue? How sad? How small?" around openings to the sky. Thus the installation works both on a practical and a spiritual level.

A light-sensitive touch panel opens the doors and, once inside, easy access is maintained. Exhibition spaces can be reached by lifts, and the two mezzanine floors by chairlift. There is a disabled person's toilet on the ground-floor. The only remaining inaccessible areas are the Egyptian gallery on the top floor, and the monumental stairways.

As part of the Harris's equal opportunities policy each part of the exhibition programme is looked at with regard to access and a Preston-based access committee regularly gives advice. William Kirby — a blind consultant in art and design for visually impaired people, former senior art lecturer and current vice chairman of the Living Paintings Trust (see page 17) — produced tactile relief maps of the whole museum, together with an audio guide. This makes the Harris the first gallery to provide a service which enables visually impaired visitors to follow where they are going while listening to taped information (see page 47).

The Old Town Hall Arts Centre, Havant

The centre has a lively programme of theatre, music, film and visual art. Its contemporary art gallery, which opened in July 1989, houses up to 10 exhibitions a year, including touring and community arts. With a high percentage of its visitors being elderly or disabled, the centre has made great efforts to improve access over recent years. Havant was the first small community arts centre in the south of England to install an induction loop system in its lecture theatre.

In 1990, prior to the opening of and exhibition of work by visually impaired artists entitled *More than Meets the Eye* (see page 33),

director Paul Sadler approached Portsmouth-based The Arts Connection (see page 33) to seek advice on ways of improving access and involving disabled people throughout the Old Town Hall's programme of activities. Recommendations included developing the gallery space, constructing a new accessible entrance and installing adapted toilet facilities.

Disabled consultants Lynn Legge of The Arts Connection, William Kirby (see page 47) and Keith May were employed to ensure that these adaptations would be of a high standard. They also made further recommendations such as installing a low-level telephone and additional handrails. The consultants keep up their dialogue with the centre, thus ensuring access is both maintained and improved.

The centre also features reserved parking for disabled people located close to the main entrance with level access; a second entrance on a higher level reached via a gentle incline; steps with white edges to guide visually impaired people, and clearly sign-posted directions to all areas. In the lecture theatre there is ample wheelchair space and wheelchair users can sit next to their companions. Guide dogs are welcome. Seating is provided in the main gallery area.

Museum of Science and Industry, Manchester

Voted "Museum of the Year" in 1990, this busy public venue has a ramp system dominating its central space. Designed to provide access and visibility to the upper floors, it is wide and gently sloping, with frequent resting platforms. A state-of-the-art lift is provided as an alternative. Both access design solutions earned the museum a commendation from the Royal Institute of British Architects in 1991.

Access for Disabled People to Art Premises Today (ADAPT)

ADAPT is a grant aid scheme, set up in 1990 with the purpose of changing buildings – and with that public attitudes – to become user-friendly to disabled people. It evolved out of the Attenborough Committee and Carnegie Council recommendations for achieving maximum accessibility by encouraging

Internal ramp system, Museum of Science and Industry

Parking for disabled people at the front of the building with level access to the main entrance of City Museum and Art Gallery, Stoke-on-Trent

Low-level public telephone with induction coupler, situated in a quiet area of the foyer, with shelf and folding seat

the involvement of government, trusts, corporate and community organisations. The overriding objective of the scheme is to challenge venue owners and managers to think about essential improvements, to plan for these within their resources, as well as ensuring that such improvements are models of good practice.

ADAPT was started with £250,000 from Carnegie (UK) Trust and the government added a further £150,000 through the Minister for the Arts. Further support came from the Esmee Fairbairn Charitable Trust, the Clothworkers Foundation and trade unions.

ADAPT makes grants available to arts venues wanting to adapt and provide facilities which benefit disabled people outside and inside buildings. Up to 50 per cent of the total costs will be met, the maximum being £25,000 and the minimum £2,000. Applicants are expected to make up the shortfall from their own or donated sources. Grants are not given to new venues since it is mandatory under current building regulations for such venues to be accessible.

ADAPT strongly recommends that the advice of disabled people be sought throughout the process of design and adaptation, and it insists that any changes must enable disabled people to follow the same route as everybody else, rather than them being segregated through "special" arrangements.

Helpful guidance notes on access are available from ADAPT. They give advice on physical features such as signposting, car parks, pavement levels, handrails, seating and toilet facilities, and on less obvious facilities like induction loops, tape guides, sign language interpretation, lighting, labelling, publicity and information.

ADAPT is administered part-time by Derek Lodge and chaired by Emma Nicholson MP, who herself has experience of disability. Its advisory committee comprises mainly representatives who are disabled and have knowledge and experience of the arts and the problems of access. The Carnegie (UK) Trust provides the administration costs of the committee so that all monies raised are

used fully and directly for grants.

In 1991, more than £1 million was spent on 60 art venues to improve access, nearly half of which came from ADAPT. A separate ADAPT Fund exists in Northern Ireland.

British Gas, in association with ADAPT, runs a series of annual awards for venues providing the best facilities for disabled people, with seven categories including arts centres, museums and galleries, each carrying a prize of £2,500, with an overall winner receiving £5,000.

City Museum and Art Gallery, Stoke-on-Trent

Built by the local authority in the mid-1950s, the museum underwent major rebuilding and refurbishments in 1981 and subsequently won the Museum of the Year Award in 1982. Situated in the heart of Stoke-on-Trent, it houses one of the largest collections of pottery and porcelain in the world, in addition to a natural history gallery, and two fine-art galleries which show touring exhibitions. A sculpture court which can be viewed from all levels of the museum and displays contemporary sculptural work is also used for performance and as studio space for artists-in-residence.

In 1988, an access working party was set up in the museum to improve physical access. Substantial improvements were made to the building and have continued since, as a result of regular consultation with disabled visitors and a number of museum staff who are registered disabled.

There are parking bays for disabled people outside the main and rear entrances, the latter approachable by a level wide pathway which also links to the road at the front. The museum can arrange transport to and from gallery events for disabled people who have no means of travelling there. The main entrance has a gentle ramp up to the doors and staff are always on hand to assist those unable to operate the manual doors. Inside, the reception counter has been lowered and space between shop displays has been widened for the benefit of wheelchair users. A rest-cum-changing room is situated nearby.

Improvements which aid visually impaired visitors include clearer signage throughout the building to aid orientation; any steps are outlined in white and have a handrail for guidance; a drinking bowl is provided for guide dogs, and personal stereos are available for taped gallery tours produced by Sound Alive and funded by the Friends of the Museum. Lighting on stairs and in dark display areas is enhanced.

Hanging heights and labelling of exhibitions are all low level for the benefit of wheelchair users and children. Large print is always used for labels and interpretive panels. Galleries on the upper levels are accessible to wheelchair users by a passenger lift which has controls in both bold digits and braille.

For deaf and partially deaf people, the telephone in the foyer is fitted with an induction coupler and an induction loop is provided in the lecture theatre. Sign language interpretation for lectures is also arranged.

The foyer telephone has a folding seat which allows access for wheelchairs, and a shelf for change and bags leaves arms free. It is sited in a quiet corner and is well signposted. Chairs in the foyer were chosen in bright contrasting colours so as to be clearly visible. Some low, soft, armless chairs have been replaced by firm high-backed ones with arms for the comfort of those with back and knee problems.

Access is incorporated in the museum's marketing strategy. The general information leaflet covers access facilities such as those listed above, the location of disabled persons' toilets and touch displays, and the availability of two wheelchairs. The quarterly museum bulletin also contains detailed access information and uses the nationally recognised symbols. All publicity material for events is mailed out to local disabled people's organisations and press.

The museum was highly commended in the category of Best Provision for Disabled Visitors, including blind people, in the Gulbenkian Museum and Gallery Awards 1990.

The museum has built up close links with local disability groups, local industry and other interested parties for assistance with its work. Its premises are used regularly for meetings and workshops by Stoke-on-Trent Disability Arts Forum and Artlink, the local Shape agency (see page 58).

In February 1990, the museum's access working party was replaced by an equal opportunities working party to look at access issues on a social as well as physical basis. A policy was drawn up to incorporate physical access with access to exhibition programming and events. The equal opportunities policy included research to determine the most appropriate means of achieving objectives, on-going consultation and monitoring, and procedures for implementation. Crucial in this was continued Disability Awareness and Equality Training for staff at all levels.

A large part of the museum's arts programme is outreach work with disabled people's groups and is aimed at empowering and encouraging them to use the museum. "Touch" workshops are also a regular feature of the exhibition programme.

To reflect the on-going commitment of the museum to equal opportunities, a major exhibition of works by disabled people was held between December 1989 and January 1990. *Art by Disabled People* comprised paintings, drawings, photographs and ceramics.

The exhibition's curator, Jim Shea, senior assistant keeper, fine-art and information, was keen to contact isolated disabled artists in the community, and did so with the aid of articles in local newspapers and on local radio, and the assistance of Artlink Newcastle. The exhibition drew large audiences and workshops were held throughout by disabled artists for disabled and non-disabled participants.

In March 1991, the sculpture court became an arena for a collaborative project involving students from Staffordshire Polytechnic (now University) and disabled people from outlying counties. Working in clay and foam rubber, a tactile sculpture was produced, for the appreciation of both visually impaired and sighted visitors.

firm foundations

It is estimated that 95 per cent of qualified architects have received no specific training in designing for the accessible built environment. Public debate on architecture still concentrates on aesthetic arguments and on form rather than function. The Roman architect Vitruvius defined architecture as being an art which answered three needs – *commoditas, firmitas, voluptas* – commodity, construction, aesthetics. As a commodity, public buildings should, foremost, be functional. To a significant number of the public, including disabled people, elderly people and parents with baby buggies, they are clearly dysfunctional.

It is no more expensive to construct accessible "user-friendly" buildings if they are designed well from the outset. New art galleries should be models of excellence, and not only in aesthetic terms. Good provision should be standard, not special.

It is estimated that 95 per cent of qualified architects have received no specific training in designing for the accessible built environment.

NUBS – Neighbourhood Use of Building and Space

NUBS is a community architecture and design practice which forms part of the technical aid team of Interchange, a national training agency and arts centre based in north London. It works throughout the Greater London area and beyond, offering a range of legal and architectural services.

Funded by the London Boroughs Grants Scheme and Camden Council, NUBS was established in 1975 with a commitment to helping community groups; voluntary organisations and non-profit-making organisations develop their own projects. It does this by providing free feasibility studies and advice on building design, adaptations and improvements, particularly for access. It has assisted many arts venues in applying for ADAPT grants (see page 39) among them Chisenhale Studios in London's East End.

Initially NUBS will discuss the requirements of the client and then translate these into a design feasibility which includes drawings, rough budget costs and a list of other experts who need to be consulted such as structural engineers and quantity surveyors. The organisation can then use this study as a basis for grant applications.

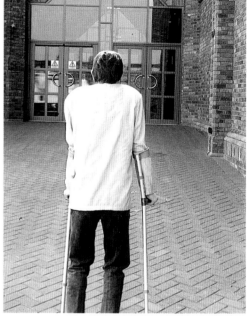

Automatic front doors at Tullie House. Photograph: Dick Capel

All Clear Designs

All Clear Designs specialises in aspects of disability and the built environment. The company works in a number of areas which range from design and construction (feasibility studies on existing and new buildings), teaching designers and issuing publications, through to Disability Equality Training for personnel. To support the above activities, the company initiates and executes a variety of research projects and pilot studies into aspects of disability, the built environment and "barrier-free" design.

Founded in January 1991, All Clear Designs has two directors, Victoria Waddington and James Holmes-Siedle. Waddington has been involved in a wide range of disability organisations in the capacity of disability researcher, outreach worker, Disability Equality Trainer and management committee member, and represents the views of disabled people on the British Standards Institute Committee overseeing the publication of *Design for All*. Holmes-Siedle uses his background in experimental psychology and design to research the needs of disabled people. Two years' experience as an ergonomist and a post-graduate diploma in the design of equipment for disabled people led to an interest in the built environment. Holmes-Siedle also has an MSc in gerontology (the study of old age), and currently serves as an adviser to the British Standards Institute and the Consumer Policy Committee on Mechanical Construction and Healthcare.

All Clear Designs' client list includes the Arts Council, the British Broadcasting Television Directorate, the Royal National Theatre, the Cockpit Theatre and the University of Brighton.

Tullie House, Carlisle City Museum and Art Gallery

Tullie House is Cumbria's largest museum and art gallery. Situated adjacent to Carlisle's Norman castle walls, it exhibits the city's archæological, art, natural and social history collections. After a total refurbishment, which incorporated access improvements to the existing Victorian Grade 1 listed building and the construction of a new wing extension, the new museum was opened in 1991.

The redevelopment scheme cost £5 million and formed part of Carlisle City Council's Urban Renaissance Scheme for the city. Civic architects worked with designers, local disability consultants and museum staff to create a venue that would be accessible to all sections of the community. Access for disabled people was written into the architects' brief and the city council's access officer advised and oversaw each stage of planning and production to ensure the brief was met.

There is level car parking space available to the side of the building, a 500-space car park four minutes away and a free coach pull-in at the front of the building. You approach the museum via a gentle slope which leads to two sets of automatic doors, purchased with an ADAPT grant (see page 39) of £6,000.

The museum is wheelchair-accessible throughout, with level access to most areas and ramps where this is not the case, such as between the old building and the new wing, and to the outdoor café terrace. A low-level telephone is located outside the café off the main concourse. Two passenger lifts give access to the upper floor

and can take 10 wheelchair users at a time. In addition, at the rear of the old building is a half-floor lift to compensate for the difference in floor levels there.

Also located in the old part of the museum, a chairlift and ramp give access to the education room. The staff, including 25 salaried gallery assistants, receive regular training on customer care and in-house Disability Awareness Training, since attitudinal access is considered as important as physical access. Staff offices have all been made accessible.

Adapted toilet facilities are situated opposite the main information desk. Fixtures such as a large mirror and soap and towel dispensers are all at wheelchair-accessible heights following repositioning after their initial installation when they were deemed impractical by users. This illustrates the museum's commitment to "getting it right", being receptive and responsive to criticism, and aware that you never achieve 100 per cent accessibility first time around.

The gallery on the ground floor is one of the biggest of its kind in the north of England, and shows national touring exhibitions of contemporary art as well as regional exhibitions. With tracked partitioning it is capable of infinite configuration to suit the nature of the work, and computer-controlled lighting can be raised to heighten visibility for groups of visually impaired visitors.

The 110-seat film and lecture theatre has two entrances, giving access to the different levels of the auditorium. Steps to the side have white toes for clear visibility. Seating is arranged to accommodate six wheelchair users, more by prior arrangement. A ramp leads to the bar and function room, and the stage is at floor level, making access to it easy for everyone. The theatre is also fitted with an induction loop system.

The museum's open exhibition spaces are well signposted and its seating areas all provide a view. Displays throughout are well-lit and at wheelchair-accessible heights. They are also well-spaced to allow wheelchair users turning room. The entire upper floor is interactive, with "hands-on" displays

The New Art Gallery at Tullie House

of historical artifacts. The whole design concept allows for flexibility and ease of redisplay.

Seventy interpretive panels located at key points throughout the museum have one-inch-high text and clear messages. Likewise, all labelling of exhibits is in large typeface, with good contrast between print and background. Audio labels are already a feature of the museum for the benefit of everyone, but in particular for print-denied and visually impaired visitors. These three-minute tapes run continually, providing information and historical anecdotes.

Director Nick Winterbotham believes no one should ever be "bored, patronised, or excluded" from any part of the museum experience. To this end, the new museum area has been designed in a way which neither disadvantages nor excludes disabled people or any other members of the community. The provision of access for disabled people, as well as baby-changing facilities and buggy park, family restaurant, film and lecture theatre, good seating and display, and an information service, are all regarded as priorities in fulfilling the museum's function of facilitating, in Winterbotham's words "the cultural enrichment of the whole community".

The Genesis Project

Genesis was founded by former teacher Jan Swain in 1987 with the aim of creating an arts centre in the heart of Sheffield designed from the outset to be totally accessible to disabled people. The first of its kind, the arts centre will eventually encompass all areas of the arts, providing space for workshops, societies, performance and exhibition. Work on the project is carried out by volunteers whose collective expertise covers areas of law, arts, disability, fundraising, publicity, education and architecture.

The building chosen for the arts centre was formally St Silas' Church Room, built at the turn of the century. Purchased with money from Yorkshire TV Telethon Trust, the building was already divided into two floors, but £250,000 worth of major alterations were required to make it totally

The Genesis building during the *Network* installation, spring 1991. Part of a trail of site-specific artworks located around Sheffield's main roads. Genesis was chosen because it widens access through continuous networking

creature comforts

accessible. There is now a lift and ramp to the first floor. Parkwood Tertiary College constructed and installed a replacement staircase designed by project architect, Mike Brearley.

When the building was first taken on it was used to mount an exhibition to introduce the project to the community and involve potential users from the outset. Since then it has served as an information drop-in centre with a "library" of disability arts literature. Located in an area of urban regeneration, the centre is accessible from main routes around Sheffield. It has its own car park to the rear alongside a large-scale wall mural created by artist Paul Wood and people from local day centres, schools and community groups.

An advisory council, a council of management, and a building committee, with a heavy representation of disabled people, guide the project. Jan Swain has generated an enormous amount of local voluntary support and interest and has forged strong links with arts and disability organisations, local schools and community groups, many of which have provided financial support.

A dance performance was held at the Lyceum Theatre, Sheffield, in March 1991 to raise further money for the project, and included performances by Common Ground Dance Theatre (an integrated disabled/non-disabled member co-operative), London Contemporary Dance and Northern Contemporary Dance School.

The Genesis project is evolving out of the community rather than being imposed on it and this gives it solid foundations. With demand and support from future arts centre users already existing through their involvement in its creation, a sense of ownership is being born.

One of the aims is to provide opportunities for both vocational and non-vocational courses in the visual and performing arts. By liaising with public and private sector organisations in arts, education and training, Genesis hopes to become a focal point for the local community, setting a good example of inner city regeneration.

Our enjoyment of visiting an art gallery or museum depends as much on our physical comfort and well-being as by what we see or experience by way of art. Many large museums and national galleries provide seating within the gallery space yet in many smaller venues it is often scarce or relegated to areas where it won't "spoil the aesthetics" of the exhibition.

We all get exhausted at exhibitions and enjoy contemplating art at leisure. Frequent rest areas and resting rails are essential. In lecture theatres and other areas of fixed seating, ample space needs to be provided for wheelchair users, bearing in mind that they don't necessarily want to be grouped together, or in the front row. Not everyone enjoys being in the firing line, not least because extra time is often needed for visits to toilet facilities, and during very short intervals this can result in visitors being delayed in returning to their places.

In disabled persons' toilets, care in positioning mirrors and other fixtures should be taken with regard to height and ease of reach, and in consultation with potential users.

At Stoke City Museum and Art Gallery (see page 40) they provide drinking bowls for guide dogs and have allowed space for dogs to lie down next to their owners during lectures or performances. Such considerations add to the overall welcome extended to the public.

Figures in Bar **by Marie Schofield, Royal National College, Hereford**

safe and soundless

Fire alarm system with flashing lights and sirens for hearing and visually impaired people – Huddleston Centre, Clapton
Photograph: Pam Usherwood, Format

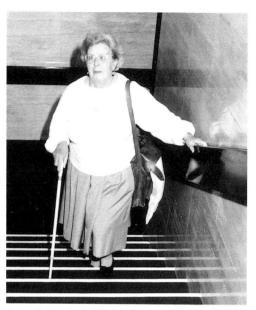

A visually impaired visitor is able to safely negotiate the stairs with the aid of white step edging and continuous handrail

The introduction of revised building regulations has brought a welcome alternative to the Cinematograph Regulations (also adopted for lecture theatres). These regulations restricted or even prohibited access or required disabled patrons to part company with their mobility aid, be it wheelchair or guide dog, implying that the people themselves were a hazard in emergency situations.

The British Standards' "Means of Escape in Case of Fire" part of the revised regulations states that "it may not be necessary to incorporate special structural measures to aid means of escape for disabled people. Management arrangements to provide assisted escape may be all that is necessary". This has obvious implications for staff training and safety procedures. Several arts venues have installed flashing light alarms for the benefit and safety of deaf patrons and staff. These need to be coupled with revised emergency evacuation procedures and practice.

For the safety of visually impaired visitors and staff, the revised building regulations suggest tactile and audible indicators for lifts, the provision of tactile, non-slip surfaces at the top of flights of stairs, and distinguishable nosing to steps. Handrails on stairs and ramps to guide you down to safety can often prove dangerous, particularly to visually impaired people, if they fail to continue to ground level. Simple solutions are often overlooked or ignored in favour of "aesthetic" rather than functional design.

Glazed panels giving a zone of visibility to enable people to see and be seen by others using the door, and vision strips on fully glazed doors are now a requirement of the building regulations, as is the directive that hazards on access routes must be illuminated if they cannot be removed.

Stoke City Museum and Art Gallery

Security guards at Stoke City Museum and Art Gallery (see page 40) have been briefed on emergency evacuation procedures and on how to assist deaf and disabled people. Although a light-flash alarm system exists to complement the sound alarm, practice emergency evacuations have taken place with volunteers from the local day centre to ensure no one's safety is compromised by being disabled.

Bubble paving stones at road crossings for the safety of visually impaired people Photograph: Ulrike Preuss, Format

the right direction

The design and layout of exhibitions and the spaces that house them should allow for independent exploration rather than create the need for guided tours. To this end, the use of tape guides, tactile relief maps and other aids to orientation such as contrasting floor texture, good hanging heights, enhanced lighting and clear signage are crucial.

Harris Museum, Preston

The audio guide to the building and collections of the Harris Museum, Preston (see page 38), was produced by William Kirby, a blind consultant in art and design. The guide provides details on distances and on floor surface to aid orientation. It also gives an idea of how rooms relate to one another and an appreciation of the architectural style. Copies can be obtained prior to visiting the gallery, to aid familiarisation with the layout, or on arrival from staff at the front desk. The Harris also produces tapes to individual exhibitions.

To launch the audio guide of the museum an exhibition entitled *A New View* was organised by William Kirby. In 1990, a selection of tactile art-works, bold line drawings and paintings that could be appreciated by people with some useful sight formed part of an exhibition entitled *Hands On* for which a tape guide was also supplied. Works were set on low plinths around which seating and low-level tables were placed, and all had a large, bold-print information card with a corresponding line drawing of the exhibit to aid identification. Both the tape guide and the exhibition were sponsored by British Telecom and gloves for handling works were donated by Boots the Chemist.

Tate Gallery, Liverpool

For the Tate's *New Light on Sculpture*, 1990–91 (see page 13), exhibits were silhouetted against the gallery walls to provide high contrast and visibility. While some pieces of work were set at floor level allowing physical as well as contemplative exploration, others were set on wide plinths enabling people to rest their elbows while looking at the work. Painted grey rather than white to avoid reflection or glare, they were sur-rounded by textured carpet squares to aid orientation.

Audio information gave details about the artists, the artworks and the working methods employed in their execution. A wall-mounted, raised tactile map aided orientation around the exhibition, which was laid out to give wheelchair users and others ample space.

Greenwich Citizens Gallery

It Makes Sense, 1989 (see page 8), a multi-sensory exhibition, was laid out in three circular routes. These were defined by rope guides and bubble carpet tracking. The carpet was laid face down so that it crackled when walked on. These aids to orientation stopped when a waist-high plinth was reached. On each plinth were details concerning the next artwork, such as where it was sited, the material, title and artist, and a guide to touching where needed, e.g. whether gentle touching was required. Signs in large black print were mounted on white foam board and attached to triangular mounts. Here the same sign was also presented in braille at an angle of 45 degrees to ease reading (signs mounted flat against the wall create a sharp angle between hand and arm tiring the wrist easily).

Clear and creatively designed signage at Bradford Community Arts Centre aids orientation. Photograph: In-Valid

Hands On **exhibition**

Photographs: Ian Wolfenden

a better reception

Right: Sunday talk at the Serpentine Gallery during the exhibition *Like Nothing Else in Tennessee*. With guest speaker Michael Archer (left facing) and sign interpreter, artist Ben Steiner (right facing). Photograph: Emma Ayling

Just as steps are barriers to wheelchair users so communication and attitudes are barriers for deaf people. Front-of-house staff are the first point of contact of any organisation and it is important that they reflect its standards and attitudes and have received Disability Awareness Training and, ideally, Deaf Awareness Training.

There are two million hearing-aid users in this country who have some degree of hearing. Many people who are totally deaf are skilled lip readers. In either case, it is important to know how to communicate effectively, i.e. by not shouting but speaking clearly, rephrasing if you have to repeat, and writing things down if necessary.

Over recent years there has been an increase in the use of communication aids for deaf people. All arts and other public venues should have an induction loop or infra-red system to allow hearing-aid users to receive loop transmissions by switching to the "T" position on their hearing aid. Likewise, induction couplers can be fitted to telephones to assist hearing, again hearing-aid users switch to "T". Telephones should always be sited in a quiet area, preferably with an acoustic hood to minimise outside interference.

Once initial expenditure has been made for basic induction loop equipment, extending the system to cover other areas of the building such as the foyer, bar or restaurant costs relatively little. A small loop and microphone can be easily installed around the box office window. Such systems are already in operation in many public places, i.e. British Rail booking offices and council rent offices. Such systems do require regular servicing and testing, and should also be advertised in publicity material by displaying the standard sign (supplied by the Royal National Institute for Deaf People). Sign-interpreted gallery talks, tours and events are being programmed more frequently, and because of this there is a growing demand for Deaf Awareness Training.

Service Call Transmitter

This is intended for use by disabled drivers, wheelchair users and others who cannot gain access to buildings because of barriers such as steps or heavy doors. The visitor points a remote-controlled transmitter at the venue, which has a receiver in its window, then presses a button. The receiver picks up the signal and a flashing light indicates that the message has been received. A buzzer sounds several times inside the building alerting a member of staff that assistance is required. While not an ideal access solution, until all public buildings are required to be accessible by law it does offer a degree of independence and an alternative to the humiliation of being left out in the cold.

Hand Shapes: A Guide to Using Sign Language Interpreters in the Arts

The aim of this guide is to institute good practice across the whole spectrum of the arts by encouraging staff to increase the accessibility of their events to deaf and partially deaf people. The book explains how sign language was banned in 1880 and subsequently re-emerged as a "different" language for a linguistic minority who have their own history and culture. It goes on to look at who uses sign language, how to choose, book and what to pay an interpreter. Importantly, it suggests ways of monitoring and evaluating the service.

General guidelines include how to communicate with deaf people, how to gear publicity to a deaf audience, and the recognised symbols to indicate availability of services and access provision such as induction loop, front-of-house facilities, text telephones such as minicom and flash-light alarms. The appendices contain a code of practice, suggested reading list, and useful addresses. It is published by Shape London, edited by Clare Davis and designed by deaf graphic artist Emma Iliffe (priced £5).

Deaf Visual Arts Forum

Formed in 1991, the Deaf Visual Arts Forum allows deaf people the opportunity to work alongside hearing people to improve access to the visual arts for deaf and partially deaf people in London. The impetus came from staff at London's Hayward Gallery, and Deaf Awareness Trainer and former visual arts teacher Laraine Callow of "Deafworks".

The forum is a loosely affiliated group of education officers from London galleries and museums including the Royal Academy, the Tate, the Photographers Gallery, the National Portrait Gallery, the Whitechapel Art Gallery and the Museum of Moving Image. It has evolved as a grassroots movement out of a wish to share good practice and resources, and to move forward together. Regular events organised by Forum members include sign-interpreted exhibition tours, in-house Deaf Awareness Training with workshops covering such topics as advertising to the deaf market, improving access, and gallery education for deaf children.

Pauline & Geraldine: Two sisters signing **by David Hevey from** *Beyond the Barriers*

know it all

Accurate information on access to museums, galleries and events gives disabled people choice and control and allows them to make pre-visit arrangements where necessary. It is important to know not only of accommodating, accessible facilities, but also of bad features or barriers that may exist.

Many access guides have been published over the years, but to be of real use they need to have been researched by disabled people themselves, constantly updated and presented in a variety of accessible formats. Accurate access information should be included in all venue publicity and there are recognised standardised symbols which could be used, such as Letraset symbols (sheet IL5207, available in art supplies shops).

An alternative and up-to-the-minute method of providing access information is via databanks and services such as Artsline, London (see page 51). There is a growing need for a national network of services and regional information points such as this. Access guides and access audits are also useful in that they can provoke further improvements since they highlight gaps in provision and raise awareness of the needs of disabled people.

Arts Access

Set up four years ago, Arts Access provides information on access to arts venues throughout Britain. Sponsored by NatWest plc, and in collaboration with British Telecom, it compiles listings for inclusion in BT's Business and Services Telephone Directories. Information is collated by means of venue visits by disabled researchers and by telephone questionnaires, and is updated annually.

Arts Access presents an annual award to the venue that has demonstrated the greatest awareness of disability access issues. The Sainsbury Wing of the National Gallery won the award in 1992 and with it an electric wheelchair for visitor use.

Access to Information and Reading Services (AIRS)

AIRS was established in 1987 in response to the need for access to information and choice for print-denied people, including visually impaired, dyslexic, illiterate and photophobic people, and those physically unable to turn pages. It produces Europe's only daily talking newspaper, *Focus*, which has over 1,000 subscribers who pay less than a pound a week to receive the service.

Operating as part of Gateshead Libraries and Arts, it has a full newsroom, three recording studios and employs 30 staff, over half of whom are disabled. *Focus* comprises a 60-minute audio tape with international, national and regional news items. The B-side of the tape includes features on gardening, fashion, history and the arts, and outside broadcasts. A weekend supplement covers topical subjects in more depth and has a "what's on" guide for the region.

In addition to *Focus,* AIRS provides a free "talking" information service giving comprehensive coverage of subjects such as civil rights, money, health and arts, including information of Gateshead Libraries and Arts' own arts programme and details of touch and multi-sensory exhibitions. AIRS also carries out transcriptions of print to tape, large print and braille, and braille to print. It makes a modest charge for such services, which helps to generate income to offset the running costs of the newspaper service. Grants from the European Social Fund have ensured the continuation of AIRS and the service has recently been extended nationally.

Equal Arts and the Arts Access Audit

Equal Arts (formerly Northern Shape) is the regional arts development agency for Cumbria, Cleveland, Tyne and Wear, Northumberland and County Durham. Revenue funded by Northern Arts, it works primarily with Local Arts Development Agencies (LADAs) with the objective of empowering disabled people and other disadvantaged groups by creating greater access to employment, training, participation, information and awareness.

As part of its commitment to increase access to the arts, it initiated a two-year Arts Access Audit of key art organisations in Newcastle city. Equal Arts felt it crucial that the audit be informed, influenced and led by disabled people and so a forum was established, comprising access officer David Burdus, Mary Curren from Newcastle Disability Forum, Alison Duddy of Broken Wing Arts Group, Julie Storey – sign language tutor and drama practitioner – and Maggie Goodbarn of AIRS.

An induction period, which included training with disability arts consultant Geof Armstrong, gave members the opportunity to discuss the structure and policy of arts organisations and the role of the audit. An access seminar was held at Northern Arts in 1990 to introduce the aims, objectives and philosophy of the audit to the arts organisations themselves. Each of the organisations then received an Arts Access questionnaire, which gave an initial assessment of both internal access (employment, training, publicity, management structure) and physical access.

Forum members then undertook visits to 12 venues including the Laing Art Gallery, Projects UK and the Tyneside Cinema, for which they received a fee. Each member completed their own questionnaire and prepared a written report. This was followed by a return visit after a six-week period for the organisation to discuss the findings and recommendations from the audit.

An integral part of the follow-up process is a programme of Disability Equality Training (DET) organised by University of Northumbria at Newcastle Arts Management Centre for staff from the audited venues.

Access to the Arts

This is a guide to arts venues in the Eastern region produced and published by the Eastern Arts Board in collaboration with Shape East (now Artlink East) at a cost of £10,000. In February 1990, a working party of disabled people was established and produced a questionnaire that was sent out to 400 venues in the region. Following the compilation of the results, four disabled researchers were appointed, and between them they visited 100 strategic venues with a set of questions to establish attitudinal as well as physical access.

This information was collated and then edited by Lucy Gampell of Shape East in collaboration with the researchers who decided the content, format and layout of the questionnaire. The result was a 140-page paperback easy-to-use handbook. The guide is available from the Eastern Arts Board, priced £2.50.

Artsline

Set up in 1981 through Capital Radio, this London-wide information and advice service on arts and entertainment for disabled people provides details on accessibility of venues, sign-interpreted plays, touch exhibitions and other events in the field of disability arts. Funded by the London Boroughs Grants Scheme, the London Borough of Camden, British Petroleum and the London Arts Board, and run by four full-time, three part-time and three volunteer workers, it answers approximately 10,000 enquiries a year.

Arts Special Info (ASI)

ASI is a database that enables the flow of information between artists, arts organisations, community and disabled people's groups wishing to set up art projects throughout Strathclyde. Launched in October 1991, the project was designed to generate interest in cultural activities, as well as encourage and facilitate arts involvement at grassroots level.

ASI has drawn together an extensive cross-section of arts contacts, skills, advice, resources and equipment in the region into an accessible network. Those wanting information write to or telephone the ASI office, at Glasgow University, and are then sent a print-out of data. Information on the database is constantly updated. It is gathered by questionnaires from arts personnel, disability groups, and regional and national contacts.

Currently holding 1,000 entries, the database cost nearly £100,000 and was funded by the European Commission, EUCREA (see page 58), Strathclyde Regional Council and private trusts.

The idea for ASI evolved because there existed no cohesive link between arts projects involving disabled people in the area, and no structure for accessing information, resources and

"By providing people with the information to set up arts projects themselves, rather than being dependent on external bodies, disabled people will be able to heighten their own profile, and this in turn will ease their integration into the mainstream artworld."
Josephine Gammell, Co-ordinator

Equal Arts Access Forum members David Burdas and Maggie Goodbarn on an Arts Access Audit visit to the Laing Gallery, Newcastle. Photograph: Keith Pattison

ADLIB

ARTGROUPS YOU COULD JOIN

ARTS VENUES (INCLUDING ACCESS)

PRACTISING ARTISTS

LINES OPEN WED - FRI 11AM - 3PM

Artshare Avon also operates an information service called Ad Lib, Arts and Disability Local Information Bank. This phone-line provides information on access to venues; disability arts groups and projects and artists

contacts, making it difficult to initiate ideas or evaluate projects. The ASI initiative is seen as a crucial one in the field of arts and disability, since it provides a common reference point and a means of sharing experience and resources.

Artshare Avon

Following the "After Attenborough" Report in 1988, which criticised the lack of action by central and local government to improve access to the arts for disabled people, Artshare South West, an off-shoot of South West Arts, commissioned a survey to investigate local needs, opportunities and policies concerning disabled people in the arts. In 1988, it appointed Diana Porter, an arts consultant with extensive experience of local arts projects, and Julie Knight, a disabled art graduate, as researchers. A working party of disabled people was set up to guide and monitor the project and carry out various elements of the research.

The aims of the survey were to make recommendations on how disabled people could be more fully involved and empowered to take part in all aspects of local arts activity. Unlike previous access surveys, the Artshare survey addressed the major issues that limit or prohibit the involvement of disabled people in the arts, such as discriminatory practice, lack of transport facilities, and segregated "special" provision.

The published report, *Disabled People are Everywhere – Let Us In!* pointed to a lack of awareness in virtually every area under investigation. In most cases there was a willingness to improve the situation, accompanied by a lack of knowledge of what to do, where to start, and how to fund improvements. Where equal opportunities policies existed, there was no cohesive code of practice relating to disability, no training for staff and no means of monitoring implementation.

The report clearly identified the need for advocating change in the arts by providing advice, information, and Disability Equality Training. Artshare Avon, a branch of Artshare South West, exists to implement these recommendations.

Based in Bristol since 1983, Artshare Avon is disabled-led and has a team of three paid workers — a co-ordinator, administrator and access researcher. Its premises, a former police station, were made fully accessible with limited funding. The entrance and floors were levelled, and plugs, light switches and other fittings were altered to accessible heights. A police cell was transformed into an adapted toilet.

Artshare Avon has a semi-political function, seeking to make an impact on art service provision in the county by advocating models of good practice, and lobbying for disability to be on every agenda. It forms a bridge between disabled people and arts pro-viders, enabling disabled people to become involved at every stage of the decision-making process.

Artshare Avon also operates an information service called Ad Lib, Arts and Disability Local Information Bank. This phone-line provides informa-tion on access to venues; disability arts groups and projects; artists, both disabled and non-disabled with experience of disability.

Its quarterly newsletter, *Ad Lib News*, promotes and publicises disability arts and arts and disability. With an eight-page format and large print and illustrations throughout, it includes a "what's on" for the region and is distributed to disabled people in the community, to disability organisations and to arts officers, local authorities and artists.

Artshare Avon also provides an access consultancy service. In 1991, in order to highlight access issues and bring them to the public arena, it commissioned a mobile photographic exhibition. Images were based on visits by a group of disabled people to a selection of art venues in Bristol and Bath, with examples of both good and bad access. The exhibition served to raise awareness and prompt action and debate.

Disability Equality Training, both in-house and in venues, is another area of Artshare Avon's work and one which it sees as being a practical and direct move towards ending discriminatory practice, in line with its ultimate aim of securing an equal share of opportunities in the arts for disabled people.

4 | **ways in ways out**

getting there

The public transport system in this country was developed to get the workforce to work. This workforce did not include disabled people. Now that it does, equal opportunities permitting, we are left with an outmoded system which is unacceptably inaccessible to a significant number of the "public".

In the late 1980s, the European Conference of Ministers of Transport's Working Party stated that 7.3 per cent of the population of Britain cannot use the existing public bus service. Disabled travellers with British Rail often fare little better, still occasionally relegated to the goods van.

Transport, "the key to freedom" for many, is regarded as a major barrier to participating in the arts, as audience or administrator. Until the mid-1980s many regional arts associations (now boards) ran transport subsidy schemes for groups attending arts events. These have largely been discontinued as a result of financial cuts.

Some organisations such as Shape and Artlink organise transport as part of a ticket or escort scheme. Others, like CRAB (see page 26), provide their own accessible transport or can arrange and help pay for transport facilities but provision like this remains scarce.

The Campaign for Accessible Transport, an organisation of disabled people, uses direct action in the form of demonstrations and the blockading of traffic arteries as a means of protest and public awareness raising. Its activists are merely exercising their civil rights in refusing to be imprisoned any longer by a transport system designed for non-disabled people.

The manifesto of Dial-a-Ride and Taxicard Users (DaRT) – transport services for disabled people – which called for fully accessible public transport, was supported by 81 London parliamentary candidates before the 1992 general election. However, it would need the Secretary of State for Transport's endorsement, and legislative enforcement, if local councils and transport authorities are to be made to tackle the problem. In the meantime, disabled people must rely on (restricted) Dial-a-Ride and Taxicard services, and

Gallery visitor and escort

the goodwill of friends and the few arts organisations who recognise that "mobility problems" are not a personal issue but a public and political one.

Artlink, Edinburgh and the Lothians

This organisation exists to encourage active participation in the arts by disabled people throughout Edinburgh and the Lothians by taking art to day centres, adult training centres, hospitals and community settings, and by providing an escort service. It receives financial support from Edinburgh District and Lothian Regional Councils, the Scottish Arts Council, various trusts, plus business and private donations. It also pursues a rigorous policy of fundraising to allow its vital work to continue and develop.

The escort service was set up in 1984, following Artlink's survey of access to Edinburgh arts venues. Since then it has grown dramatically and currently has over 100 volunteers and 200 clients. Extra staff are recruited for the annual Edinburgh Fringe Festival and in 1991 nearly 700 outings were organised.

Clients are matched with volunteers who share similar interests, and the latter then accompany the client to arts events of the client's own choosing. Artlink organises the booking of tickets (negotiating with venue managers for concessionary rates), ensures seats are accessible for their client's needs and arranges transportation.

All volunteers are interviewed and have to provide references, they then receive induction and in-service training. They get together regularly with staff, other volunteers and clients to discuss any difficulties they have encountered, and receive practical advice and guidance from the clients themselves.

Ticket Schemes

Various organisations have schemes whereby they arrange tickets for and accompaniment to exhibitions, theatres and concerts.

Andrea Lamb, who is visually impaired, has been running Artlink, West Yorkshire's ticket scheme, since 1987 (see page 73). The service covers a wide geographical area, and is advertised in newspapers, on local radio, and by leaflet distribution to libraries, hospitals, clinics and other community venues. Since 1991, the scheme has expanded enormously, attracting many new members and volunteers. This rapid growth has, however, highlighted the need for appropriate transportation to venues through community transport, access buses and accessible taxis.

The Shape ticket scheme has been going for over a decade and enables disabled and elderly people to visit exhibitions and performances in London which they would otherwise have no access to. Shape arranges reduced-price tickets to theatre events, exhibitions and concerts for members, their friends, relatives and escorts. Practical arrangements such as ensuring suitable seating is available and organising volunteer drivers and escorts, are also part of the service. The annual cost of membership is £7.50 to individuals and £15 to groups. Included in this subscription is a bi-monthly "what's on" style newsletter, also available in tape format. Membership currently stands at around 600 although as groups constitute a third of this total, potential users number around 5,000.

East End Arts Access started up in 1990 when Glasgow was European City of Culture. The organisation provides a ticket booking and escort service intended to give housebound or mobility-impaired residents of the east end of Glasgow access to arts events. With funding from Glasgow City Council, the East End Initiative (set up to regenerate the east end), and Citibank, it also organises and pays for transport to and from venues.

Rush Hour at Aldgate East by **Sally Booth**

well connected

Many organisations exist to work and develop links with others in the arts both at home and abroad. Working in mainstream art venues, with professional artists, arts officers and administrators, and in the community, these organisations seek to improve awareness and provision for disabled people.

The Arts Connection

Formerly Solent Art Link and then Artlink South, The Arts Connection was established in 1985 to create access to arts provision and develop links between mainstream and community-based arts activity throughout Hampshire. By 1987, it had extended into West Sussex and the Isle of Wight in response to demand. It employs six workers and policy is set by a board of directors, half of whom are disabled. Extra support is provided by volunteers, who in the past have included disabled people and people with learning difficulties.

The organisation works with people of all ages who are outside mainstream arts provision because they have limited access to it. These include disabled people, people with learning difficulties, people recovering from mental illness and those who are severely socially disadvantaged.

The Arts Connection organises projects which respond to participants' expressed needs, contracting-in professional artists to share their skills through practical workshops. Wherever possible, projects take place in mainstream venues such as art centres, colleges and community centres. Director Richard Wiczkowski believes that hiring space does not effect change, whereas working in partnership with venues where disability issues are discussed and provision is negotiated, often does.

Part of The Arts Connection's role is lobbying for improved access and opportunity in mainstream arts. To this end it arranges projects and residencies, working with staff and students in colleges of fine art, extending provision to meet the needs of disabled people and encouraging collaborative work. It has also curated and promoted a number of exhibitions (see page 33).

In furtherance of its work on access in the region, The Arts Connection published an access guide in 1989. To produce the guide researchers visited arts venues throughout the Hampshire area to assess their facilities for disabled people. The

Participants, *Myths and Legends* festival, The Ark, 1991.

organisation is also involved in advisory work and employs a number of disabled consultants, among them William Kirby (see page 47), who lend specialist help on issues of access and adaptation. It also provides arts-based Disability Awareness Training to venues to ensure "access" is more than just physical, but incorporates staff attitudes and employment practice.

Projects arranged by The Arts Connection have included a 12-week silkscreen printing project at Brookside Day Centre for adults with learning difficulties (1986) and a five-day art and dance residency at Mordaunt School, Southampton (1989). In the latter project, children with physical impairments and learning difficulties worked alongside a sculptor and the London Contemporary Dance Education Team to create a mixed media environment, where they could explore visual artwork using scented paints and other materials.

In 1990, a sculpture, printing and painting project engaged Gambolling Guizers — an integrated dance/mime theatre company, a visual artist and a musician — in a one-week residency at Hawth Arts Centre, Crawley. This involved teenagers with learning difficulties and pupils from the local comprehensive school in the production of a spectacular sculptural environment and performance.

The Ark

Eight years ago, peripatetic performer Penny Sanderson founded The Ark at Bracknell's South Hill Park, one of the country's largest art centres, to assist access to the arts for people with learning difficulties. As director of the project, her overriding aim was to facilitate their full participation as creators, performers, spectators and decision-makers at the centre thus ensuring they received the same quality of experience as other members of the community.

Intrinsic to The Ark's working practice is an acceptance that everybody's contribution, based upon individual perceptions and interpretations, is both valid and valuable. As Sanderson says: "Art is the only facility I know that can offer people with learning difficulties the opportunity to express their own view of the world. For disempowered people with few words at their disposal, music, dance, drama and visual arts provide an alternative vocabulary and the chance to become eloquent."

The Ark uses every area of the arts centre, from the jewellery and pottery studios to the recital room and theatre. The Ark's own studio in the grounds of South Hill Park provides a secure, intimate setting for students and one from which all activities are centralised. "The key to our success is that we are based here," explains Penny Sanderson. All arts officers at South Hill Park are on The Ark's planning committee, helping to incorporate its work into the centre's overall programme. And because of its location, it attracts hundreds of professional artists, among them sculptors, puppeteers, ceramicists, musicians, actors, dancers and film-makers, all wanting to share their wide-ranging skills.

The Ark has an annual budget of around £60,000. It is project- and revenue-funded by the Southern Arts Board which also support an administrative post. Additional funding from the Arts Council and local authorities, plus substantial voluntary supports, allows the organisation to extend its workshop programme.

In any given week up to 30 artists and about 100 students with learning difficulties — from schools, day centres and hospitals — are involved in The Ark. The organisation also runs workshops, special projects, performance events, full-time residencies and training sessions for artists and staff from social services, health and education authorities.

The culmination of each year's activities for The Ark is the summer festival. Set in South Hill Park's Wilde Theatre and embracing all the centre's resources, the festival is a collaborative performance and a fusion of art forms. (The Wilde Theatre has removable stalls to give a wide flooring area which extends to the stage at the same level. Flexible level staging provides an ideal arena for the festivals, since there is no performer–audience divide and

The Sun God from *Myths and Legends*

everyone can be actively involved.)

Every year the festival is based on a carefully selected theme around which the year's workshops are built. This means that over a 12-month period, all of The Ark's participating groups gain a sense of continuity and common purpose — it also allows visiting artists to work within a clearly defined context.

Past themes have included the elements, planets and banquets. The 1991 festival was based on myths and legends. An 18-foot tall straw "Sun Man" sculpture sat centre stage. Created by students working with Marcel Baettig, a sculptor from east London, it represented the Inca Sun God.

All other activities took place around him. Led by Common Ground Dance Theatre, imaginary journeys taken on "magic carpets" linked sub-themes of different cultures creating a moving picture. These journeys took in myths from the Far East, Europe and South America. Bamboo and gourd instruments were played alongside the pan pipes of Chilean musicians, bringing the visual images to life. Animated sculptures and giant masks created by students and Forkbeard Fantasy Comic Theatre Company were rolled on and off stage, and symbolised four aspects of the Sun Man's life — childhood and adulthood, love and work. The grand finale came when he was hoisted by crane 140 feet into the air while all participants looked on, chanting and making music.

Shape London

The Shape network is a national federation of arts development agencies whose collective aim is to extend access to high quality artwork and the arts professions to those unable to make use of existing provisions, particularly disabled and elderly people.

Shape London, the founding agency of the network and still its largest, has a programme of workshops, long- and short-term projects, training courses and placements, performances and festivals. It is geared towards the promotion of disability arts and culture and works in partnership with the London boroughs of Hackney, Hammersmith and Fulham, Islington, Wandsworth and Waltham Forest,

Shape in Malaysia

towards creating permanent improvement in provision for and by local disabled people.

Locally based arts development workers research local needs and devise projects in consultation with local groups and individuals. As a result, the arts are brought to venues such as day centres, schools, residential homes and hospitals. In 1991, there were over 100 workshops and projects in such settings, as well as events which attracted disabled people to arts centres and galleries.

Although London-based, Shape London's work extends beyond the city's boundaries. In November 1991, Guy Evans, projects co-ordinator and musician; Elspeth Morrison, drama workshop tutor and trainer; and Annora Spence, visual arts tutor, travelled to Malaysia for three weeks. There they worked with disabled people, care workers and occupational therapists through workshops in Disability Awareness Training, batik, screen and fabric printing, painting, drama and music, in settings where disabled people had little experience of arts activity.

The workshops culminated in two performances by over 50 disabled workshop participants on the main stage of Kuala Lumpar's central market. The performance attracted a high level of media and public interest, thereby raising the visibility of disabled people in the community in a positive way.

European Committee on Creativity by and for Disabled People (EUCREA)

EUCREA exists to promote the networking of disabled artists and their organisations throughout the EC. It provides one-off grants (normally up to half the total costs) to arts projects which actively involve disabled people from four or more European countries. Applications are processed by the National Disability Arts Forum (see page 31). EUCREA also gives an annual award to a disabled individual who has made an outstanding contribution to Disability Arts. Photographer Jo Spence won the award in 1991 for her work on the experience of living with cancer, which made visible the underlying reality of pain, economic non-viability and impending death.

Art to Share, Nottingham

Art to Share was founded in Nottingham in 1978 by blind art-lover Lewis Jones and Dr Sheila Smith of Nottingham University, with money from the Henry Moore Foundation. Led by a committee of eight blind and visually impaired adults, it has some 36 members and aims to enable them and sighted people to share the arts together through discussion and activity.

Art to Share has learnt by experience that fruitful and imaginative exploration of art is "killed" if a sighted person guides a visually impaired person, for instance by telling them the title of a piece of a sculpture before there has been the opportunity to explore it. Instead, Art to Share encourages an exploration of an artwork together, exchanging views and discoveries so both gain greater insight.

The organisation's yearly programme includes adult education classes, talks, practical workshops and visits to exhibitions and venues such as the Yorkshire Sculpture Park (see page 87). This aims to stimulate ideas for participants' own work, which has in the past included large-scale environmental sculpture. Members get the chance to meet and work with practising artists, among them potters, painters and sculptors. Art to Share members have collaborated with Shape, GRAEAE Theatre Company and galleries such as the Whitechapel in London (see page 15), and the Walsall Gallery in the West Midlands, which has a large collection of sculptural works by Jacob Epstein.

Transportation is a key problem for Art to Share, overcome in part by voluntary transport provision and the assistance of sighted helpers. Lewis Jones believes that through art the lives of the group are enriched, and they gain greater confidence and understanding of the world. The group is always seeking new ways of overcoming barriers to extend the experience and practice of art.

Artists Agency, Sunderland

Founded by Lucy Milton in 1983, Artists Agency organises artist placements in health and community settings, in prisons and in industrial sites. Operating across Cleveland, Cumbria, Durham, Northumberland and Tyne and Wear, with funding from Northern Arts, it has organised over 60 placements to date.

Some, like the Art Studio (see page 34), have established themselves as autonomous projects, and many have gained wide recognition, winning

Lynne Otter (1991). This work is a personal view of beauty and danger, an eloquent representation of uncertainty and tension in the AIDS years. From *Living Proof*, produced during the Artists Agency HIV/AIDS project

national awards. In 1986, Artists Agency won the ABSA Art Award "for outstanding use of commercial sponsorship in the arts" and the Artworks for Industry Award for a series of commissions and exhibitions in industrial sites. In 1987, it received the Art and Work Award "for best public site-specific artwork in Britain".

Artists Agency believes that because art is a social and personal activity, as well as a vital force within society, artists should be encouraged to work in social settings. It pioneers new ways of enabling practising artists to work with people and communities who have had little or no contact with art, believing that both parties can benefit from this interaction. "It can extend and deepen the artist's work and give those who work with them a chance to develop their talents and enjoy their own creativity," says founder Lucy Milton.

In recent years, Artists Agency has sought to address the issues facing people with HIV and AIDS, since those affected come up against similar taboos, social barriers and misrepresentations as disabled people. As Esther Salamon of Artists Agency explains: "AIDS has become a way to justify existing social mores and a means to reinforce socially divisive attitudes, prejudices and inequalities. In order to move beyond these two-dimensional views of a complex issue there is a need to create imagery, metaphors and perspectives which can confront the social and cultural issues surrounding the epidemic."

Thus in June 1991, Artists Agency began a major HIV/AIDS project which involved a residency and commission for photographer Nicholas Lowe and creative writer Michael McMillan. The project was designed to enable those affected by HIV and AIDS (including partners, family, friends and carers) to work with artists and through a creative approach, to express their concerns, interests, hopes and fears in their own terms. The project also drew in a host of organisations already involved with HIV/AIDS work including Cleveland AIDS Support, Outrage, Durham Prison, Newcastle Polytechnic, AIDS Community Trust, and local drug

abuse and haemophilia centres, in addition to many voluntary agencies.

Artists were able to pursue their own work, informed by the residency, and to produce visual and literary material which promoted new understanding and interpretation of the issues surrounding HIV and AIDS. These, it is hoped, have contributed to the wider debate and in so doing have helped break down existing barriers and fears.

The project also included workshops, training sessions and performances based on safer sex. People unable to attend because of the often debilitating nature of HIV, had artists visit them in their own homes or in hospital. Counselling from independent counsellors recommended by the agency Body Positive North East was available throughout the project for anyone involved and continues now the project is complete.

The work produced by artists and participants — photographic images, poetry, prose and plays — was published as a paperback book entitled *Living Proof: Views of a World Living with HIV and AIDS*, and formed two exhibitions at the Laing and Zone Galleries, Newcastle, in May 1992.

The project culminated in North East AIDS Week, a festival which brought together the whole community, urging it to take responsibility away from the artists by facing up to HIV/AIDS, and taking action. "The sum of the project is not Nick or myself, but the sum of the participants, since we as artists, as activists, have only empowered and activated many marginalised voices that already exist," says Michael McMillan.

Artwork was displayed in prominent public locations on huge hoardings carrying six contrasting images, one of which featured in the BBC 2/*Radio Times* "Commissions and Collaborations" arts season, and then went on view in 10 locations around the country.

Over £50,000 was raised for this model pilot project, and since £15,000 of this was provided by the European Commission, the project has forged links with Europe and beyond, with work subsequently going on display outside the UK.

reaching out

Non-building-based arts provide an alternative to inaccessible art venues. Many outreach programmes run by local authorities or individual galleries provide facilities whereby art is taken out to people in hospitals, homes, day centres and rural districts where art provision is scarce. Several provide fully accessible facilities allowing and encouraging full participation in the arts by disabled people, a selection of which are described here.

The Sea Chest

In 1987, Caroline Sier of Eastern Arts and Lucy Gampell of Shape East were assessing provision in the arts for visually impaired people when the idea of a sea chest packed with seaside artifacts and memorabilia emerged as a means of stimulating creative work. The theme of the seaside and coastal heritage was pertinent because of the geographical location of both organisations, and therefore likely to stimulate interest in their clients.

The cost of commissioning *Sea Chest*, around £2,000, was met by Eastern Arts Association, the Royal National Institute for the Blind, Shape East and Anglia Television Telethon Trust. Crafts workers were selected to create pieces for the *Sea Chest* and Suffolk Social Services mobility officer for the blind was consulted. He provided artists with a range of special glasses during a series of meetings, to demonstrate the different sorts of visual impairment they would have to consider when producing their work.

Each artist selected a particular aspect of the theme and these included the fishing industry, environmental issues, transport, seaside toys and sea trade. Rowan Wood, a workshop which employs people with learning difficulties and specialises in sculpture and furniture, built the chest. Working models of crabs, lobsters and a seagull which pops out of a chimney when you clap your hands, were made by Ron Fuller, and Street Forge Workshops constructed mechanical vehicles. Puppets were created by Meg Amsden and included a fishergirl, a herring and starfish, each made of highly tactile materials.

A wave machine by Tim Hunkin comprising a snare drum run on a pivot motor, with ball bearings on top, created the sound of waves rolling on a pebble beach. Jane Wells, composer-in-residence, produced a sound-tape which was installed in the chest producing evocative sea sounds, instrumental music and bird song. Natural objects such as shells, fossils and pebbles, were also added to contrast with the craft objects.

The *Sea Chest* was launched at the Whale Centre in Wells next-the-sea, Norfolk, in September 1988, with an event which incorporated the singing of sea shanties, a puppet show, music, juggling and performance. Involving full audience participation, it drew together many potential users of the chest.

Since its creation, the chest has travelled 10,000 miles and has been used by thousands of people in schools, hospitals, clubs for visually impaired people, and adult training centres, where it has sparked off hundreds of informal art, craft and music-making sessions.

Shape East, which has now restructured and is known as Artlink East, organises and funds professional artists to run workshops using the chest to stimulate creative activity. An

Sea Chest. **Photograph: Artlink East**

Sea Chest. **Photographs: Artlink East**

Photograph: Steve Marshall

The Trojan Horse at the *Festival of the Five Senses*, Hexham.
Photograph: Keith Pattison

accompanying information pack in large print and braille, and on tape, is provided to ensure maximum benefits are gained from its use. The chest is loaned free-of-charge to users within the Eastern region.

Artscope

Based in the North-east and run by artists Malcolm Smith and Steve Marshall, Artscope encourages practical participation in the visual arts through the initiation of projects and workshops throughout the whole community. Its particular commitment is to working with disabled people and others who have limited access to mainstream arts. Artscope's work is based on the sharing of skills and experience. It functions in partnership with other organisations, advising and supporting individuals to maximise their own abilities and skills. It also develops new and alternative ways of working, encouraging a participatory response to art through enhancement of the five senses.

The *Trojan Horse* is a multi-sensory sculpture, designed by Malcolm Smith and made by Artscope to stimulate sight, touch, hearing and smell, and is particularly popular with people with sensory impairments. The basic shape is recognisable and approachable, relating to the human scale. Standing seven feet tall at the head, it is five feet long and two-and-a-half feet wide. Sensory elements have been widely distributed to render them accessible to children and wheelchair users. Its surface encompasses a wide range of materials: wood, plaster, velvet, wax, metal and braille text offer a variety of textures. Small compartments and items suspended from the horse's belly can be explored by touch; olfactory elements are introduced through the use of scented materials; and sound, through bells in the bridle and tail.

The *Trojan Horse* has toured to many venues, among them galleries, schools and hospitals, where it has been used as a starting point for arts activity. It undergoes continual modification according to the users' response. Having been in heavy use since it was built in 1989, it has required constant

maintenance and replacements, and over 700 hours have been spent on its design, construction and refurbishment.

It is frequently available to a broader public. An appearance at the Metrocentre, Gateshead, followed residencies at *The Festival of the Five Senses*, Hexham (see page 11), and the *Freedom to Touch* exhibition at the Laing Art Gallery, Newcastle, both in 1989.

Kirin Saeed, a visually impaired arts administrator who undertook a traineeship with Equal Arts (see page 77) during 1990–91, made a tape guide for exploring the *Trojan Horse*. This has been used to facilitate and promote its fuller use.

The Scottish Arts Council's Travelling Gallery

The Travelling Gallery takes a range of imaginative and provocative exhibitions to locations as diverse as shopping centres, hospitals, prisons and schools from Shetland to the Borders. The service was launched in 1978 with the original vehicle replaced in 1983 by a custom-built one. A programme of workshops, lectures and other activities take place during each tour.

Virtual Realities, the 1991 summer tour exhibition, was designed to be fully accessible to blind, partially sighted and fully sighted people. The exhibits were chosen for their materials, textures, colour and subject matter. The exhibition incorporated work by the Boyle family, Ian Hamilton Finlay and Veronica Ryan. Also included in the show were photographs by artist Dosh McClure whose self-portraits explore the balance of control between being both behind and in front of the camera. Three large-scale colour photographs illustrated her feelings about being visually impaired, and conveyed the frustration, isolation and lack of control she experiences.

The exhibition was accompanied by a catalogue which combined braille and large-print text (see page 18), and a number of workshops and "hands on" elements were incorporated into the project.

Arts in Fife

Artbus, a fully accessible, self-powered travelling gallery, was launched in June 1991 by Arts in Fife, Fife Regional Council Education Department. Funded by the education department, with support from the Scottish Arts Council, the purpose-built mobile gallery tours throughout Fife visiting communities and schools.

Artbus completed a second public tour with an exhibition called *Magic Maker,* which explored the world of fantasy in art. The Artbus already has a high profile and is easily recognised by its striking exterior design. It takes exhibitions of contemporary art out to audiences, thereby increasing availability and access to the visual arts for the whole community.

The aim of Artbus is to provide a continuous programme of quality exhibitions which directly involve people. These are supplemented by a workshop programme which engages visitors in the process of making art, thereby increasing awareness and understanding.

Since the appointment of an arts and disability officer to Arts in Fife, an emphasis in this direction has been made across the programme, and Artbus reflects this. The top floor of Artbus has been removed and the ground floor raised to accommodate wheelchairs. The main double-door entrance at the rear is ramped, leading into a user-friendly art gallery space. Consideration is given to visually impaired patrons in the programming of exhibitions and workshops, and artworks are labelled in large print. Audio-taped catalogues are planned for future exhibitions.

Each exhibition makes approximately 50 public stops to hospitals, community and day centres, and over 50 visits to secondary and primary schools, with an average attendance of 25,000, which includes a high percentage of disabled people. Arts in Fife is developing links with permanent art venues and encouraging audiences to visit other art exhibitions. It is also providing the catalyst for the setting up of exhibition areas and arts programmes within establishments such as hospitals and community centres.

Community Arts Workshop (CAW), Manchester

CAW is an outreach organisation which has been working with traditionally excluded sections of the community since 1979. CAW facilitates access to

Teacher and pupil from the Blind School, Edinburgh, explore the *Virtual Realities* summer tour exhibition, 1991, SAC's Travelling Gallery. Photograph: Sean Hudson

the arts by offering community-based activities such as drama, music video and visual arts. CAW seeks to foster equal partnerships between artists and clients through the exchange of skills, knowledge and experience thus permitting work to be continued independently.

Working across the ten boroughs of Greater Manchester, it is funded by North West Arts Board, Manchester City Council and the Association of Greater Manchester Authorities.

In 1989, CAW consulted with disabled people from across Greater Manchester involved in disability arts practice with the aim of producing a disability arts policy which CAW could act upon. As a result, the following steps were taken: disabled people joined CAW's management group; positive action was taken to employ disabled practitioners resulting in the employment of two disabled workers; successful application was made for monies from the ADAPT fund (see page 39) and the Department of the Environment to make its premises more accessible for workers; CAW's marketing strategy targeted disabled people including disabled people's forums.

As part of its development role in the region, CAW has invested significant time to support the establishment of Taking Liberties, Wigan Disability Arts Forum. Taking Liberties, which has been in existence for over two years, is a group of disabled people and their allies who wish to open up opportunities to create, produce, distribute and enjoy their own art and culture. CAW continues its support in a variety of ways.

Taking Liberties' first project was an open-day event called *Run of the Mill*, held in January 1991 at the Mill at Wigan Pier. One of *Run of the Mill*'s aims was that it should bring to the attention of Wigan local authority the extent and range of interests of disabled people in the borough and thereby influence its arts policy. But principally, it sought to raise the profile of the need for arts facilities and resources for disabled people. Geared towards people aged 16 and over *Run of the Mill* created a stimulating, informative environment

where disabled people had access to a whole range of arts activities. Emphasis was placed on engaging people in the creative process, drawing attention to production possibilities, making full use of current arts technology, and avoiding stereotypical activities that are often thought of as particularly relevant to disabled people such as mask-making. The event was rounded off with an evening cabaret, featuring disabled performers.

Run of the Mill was well publicised through CAW's network of regional contacts, a local mailing list, along with ads and articles in the local press aimed at disabled people who were not part of any group. Transport for those who required it was provided by the Greater Manchester Transport Executive. The cost of the day, around £4,500, was met by North West Arts Board, Esmee Fairbane Charitable Trust, Wigan Community Chest, Mersey Basin Campaign and Telethon '90.

Ninety-five places were booked throughout the day for workshops in video, visual art, writing and music. There was also a photographic workshop which gave participants the opportunity to be photographed in the manner in which they wished to be portrayed. This was accompanied by the Camerawork touring exhibition *A Sense of Self*, by David Hevey (see page 22), based on positive representations of disabled people.

Since this event, Taking Liberties has completed a 15-week multi-media project which was open to disabled people throughout Wigan and involved workshops in computer graphics, drama, music and video.

In conjunction with Greater Manchester Coalition of Disabled People, CAW also ran a series of mixed-media workshops, out of which sprang a new young people's social club, Kulture Club, with the aim of providing the mechanism for young people, using the arts where appropriate, to determine their own social life.

Tate Gallery, Liverpool – Outreach Programme

The Tate, Liverpool, has a mobile art programme, with a team of outreach workers who take material out to people in schools or centres as a precursor to gallery visits. In 1988, a series of workshops entitled *I Can Paint* was held at the Tate as a way of introducing the experience of visual art to non-gallery goers, particularly to disabled children and adults from day centres. An exhibition of disabled children's work under the same title was held in January 1989.

As a follow-up to this gallery-based experience, outreach projects were devised with a number of the centres. Initial research and consultation identified an appropriate and meaningful context in which to carry out larger-scale projects. Beginning in April 1990, users and staff of three day centres worked with the Tate and community arts group Arts Works, on a range of arts-based activities, under the title *Expression and Engagement*.

Participants later formed The Daylight Group with its own steering committee. Through regular meetings it set out to share its experiences with a wide range of people involved in the mental health services on the Wirral through a programme of art activity, including visits to galleries, among them the Tate, Bluecoat and Open Eye, where they often worked with artists to explore exhibition work and develop their own ideas. The gallery visits were linked to workshops through which the group applied ideas to their own environment, and from making initial models and drawings, they created sculptural installations sited at the day centres.

Artsreach, London

Artsreach is Jacksons Lane Community Centre's main educational outreach project. Based in Highgate, north London, it works with disabled people, complementing the centre's work with after-school work, festivals, summer schools and vocational training across the art forms. It also serves as a testbed for new ideas and practices, such as assessment and evaluation, which can then be adapted to the rest of the centre's work. Although Artsreach is an independent project it reports to the centre's community education and

Left and below: Pupils from Vale School and The Marksfield Project, Haringey, London during the Artsreach summer school, 1988. Photographs: Nancy Willis

training committee, and its personnel are ultimately responsible to the centre's management committee.

The project ran as a pilot scheme in Haringey from 1981 to 1983 when it was funded by London's Capital Radio. Early in 1984, it was extended to work with Inner London Education Authority schools for disabled children in north London. Over the years, funding from the London Arts Board, London Boroughs Grants Scheme, Camden and Islington Councils, the Sir John Cass Foundation, Gulbenkian Foundation, Tottenham Grammar School's Foundation, and Haringey Arts Council have allowed it to continue its work of providing opportunities for children with limited access to the arts.

The central objective of Artsreach is to involve professional experienced artists in sustained work with children and teachers, taking place at Jacksons Lane and in schools for disabled children throughout its catchment area of the London boroughs of Islington, Haringey and Camden.

Work is intended to be of long-term benefit to the children; it therefore has to be part of their experience both in and out of school hours and after they leave school. They are introduced gradually to the integrated activities of Jacksons

Lane and other centres to extend their social sphere, break down their isolation and help them develop their potential. Summer schools are also held to provide continued activity throughout the school holidays.

Arts and community centres are increasingly seen as having an important role to play in complementing the work of the education sector. Artsreach's innovative work in this field has gained it national as well as local attention.

In 1991, projects of varying length took place within 15 schools, amounting to some 200 workshops, each with an average of 10–12 children. Over 20 artists were employed, five of whom were disabled. A long-term training programme for disabled artists has been started to ensure more are employed in the future.

Arts activities have included music, dance and drama, puppet-making, video production and mural construction. One project involved the making of a mural to cover an entire wall of the gym at Moselle School, Haringey, where the pupils devised the ideas, and designed and executed the work alongside an Artsreach artist.

The starting point for each project is the

teacher's perception of the group's needs and interests. A programme of work is tailormade to facilitate the fullest educational and social benefit for each individual involved, and to reflect the racial, cultural and social composition of the group, and because good relations have been established with schools over the years, Artsreach is able to be experimental.

This approach enables individuals to develop their communication skills, perception and imagination, and enhances their ability to take risks and to realise their creative potential. Artsreach believes that its work should be integrated into the National Curriculum and for this to happen effectively it works at developing links between teachers, pupils, artists and the centre. This is done by frequent meetings to discuss objectives, working methods, evaluation and feedback, and by joint workshops for artists, teachers and parents linked to the work their children are doing in school.

Between February and June 1990, Artsreach and the Institute of Education, University of London, worked on a collaborative project whereby eight post-graduate secondary education student art teachers and their tutors were introduced to the Artsreach approach. Working alongside Artsreach artists and classroom teachers in two schools for disabled children in Islington, they examined the transferability of practice and skills, and assessed the benefits of art across the curriculum.

Artsreach feels that particular art forms can be used as the means for learning in many areas of the National Curriculum, for instance, using visual arts with deaf students to develop language and mathematical awareness. An art form can also be used to develop awareness of subjects not specifically identified in the curriculum such as sexism, disability awareness and health education. A four-year pilot project at Rosemary School, Islington, examined the role of drama and the visual arts within health and sex education. Image in Action is now a well-established permanent project within the school's curriculum.

River Life (ultra violet puppetry), from *Still Waters*, Horse and Bamboo

River Cat (shadow puppet), from *Still Waters*

Horse and Bamboo, Lancashire

Horse and Bamboo is a live art company located in the Rossendale Valley, north of Manchester. Based in a foundry, it draws on the tradition of the old touring circus and travelling players, with work centred around an annual horse-drawn tour. Often hundreds of miles long, tours take innovative work to rural audiences throughout the North-west. There have also been tours to the Outer Hebrides, the Antrim coast of Northern Ireland and abroad. Horse and Bamboo is a registered charity, revenue funded by North West Arts Board, Lancashire County Council and Rossendale Borough Council.

Formed by Bob Frith in 1974, the company was inspired by painting, and at the time had no awareness of contemporary performance art or other groups working in the field. Since 1978, Horse and Bamboo has created nearly 50 performances combining theatre and visual arts, using full head masks with giant puppets, music

and narrative. Work ranges from shows made specifically for Gaelic-speaking communities to pioneering work with disabled people.

Since 1982, Horse and Bamboo has been developing a unique approach to theatre for people with learning difficulties. Known as "Guided Imagery", it creates a world of powerful stimuli, sounds, images, colours and textures through which a "journey" is taken and utilises the basic qualities of game playing.

The *Still Waters* project ran for 10 weeks in Scotland and Lancashire in 1991. Each performance involved groups of no more than 10 who took an imaginary journey by submarine into a labyrinth of underworld caves where they encountered masked characters such as the River Cat and Fortune Teller. Using simple shadow-and-stick puppetry, masks and ultraviolet lighting (particularly good for its strong sensory quality), plus live music and theatrical elements, a realistic journey was created using visual images rather than words. On each "journey into the unknown" there would be risks to take and problems to confront. These often elicited strong feelings and emotions, and challenged participants to overcome their fears. Performers and carers reassured them, particularly those with hearing or visual impairments who may have been more frightened by the experience. But ultimately by overcoming problems and making decisions, individuals returned to safety and the journey would end.

The performances were intended to stimulate the imagination, improve communication and problem-solving skills and facilitate creative exploration by multi-sensory means. To retain a strong element of surprise, staff and carers were asked not to disclose more than the bare minimum of detail in advance. Participants brought with them a small travelling bag containing objects to be used along the journey, adding to the anticipation. Pre-visit resource packs were sent out to teachers to help introduce the theme and vocabulary.

Performances were held in the morning and stimulated activity-based workshops in the afternoon. Drawing images and acting out events led to participants creating a performance of their own.

A core of five staff comprising artistic director Bob Frith, two administrators, a full-time artist and a horse handler, plus a pool of artists, devise the scripts. Solutions are sought on how to build an environment which is both accessible and stimulating, while being tailored to a group's needs. All performances are wheelchair accessible, but the booking form is geared to determining particular needs and sometimes the performance is modified to suit one individual. Follow-up questionnaires aid evaluation to enable revision and improvement of future performances and practice.

Horse and Bamboo run training courses on Guided Imagery (which has been hailed as a milestone in educational practice) for students, artists and social workers interested in working with disabled children in this way.

Fortune Teller (masked puppet) from *Still Waters*

5

and so to work

just the job

In the City by **Sally Booth**

Official figures[1] suggest that 70 per cent of disabled people of working age are jobless and that only 12 per cent of the disabled workforce hold professional or managerial positions, compared to 21 per cent of non-disabled workers. Recent research[2] has shown that only 4 per cent of employers encourage applications from disabled workers, 13 per cent will only employ them for "certain" jobs, 25 per cent might discriminate and 6 per cent will not employ disabled people "under any circumstances".

On July 26 1990, President Bush ratified the Americans with Disabilities Act (ADA), a civil rights charter for disabled people and the first of its kind in the world. It makes detailed provision for individual rights in employment, public services, transport and housing. Although it gives a flexible standard, businesses being required to do only "what is readily achievable", it does forbid any government body or employer with over 15 workers to discriminate against a qualified disabled person simply on the grounds of them being disabled. A Civil Rights Bill designed to end discriminatory practice in this country, failed during 1991.

In the UK, with a lack of employment rights for disabled people and with equal opportunities policies which bare no teeth, the legal employment quota of 3 per cent remains disproportionate to the number of disabled people in the population, yet even this target has not been reached. It has been suggested that of the half million employees in the subsidised art sector, only 100 are disabled.[3]

Equal opportunities policies in arts organisations are frequently drawn up by an external body, then set in stone and ticked off as a credit towards fulfilling funding criteria. Instead they should be working documents, fluid in nature, permeating every level of an organisation's structure and practice, constantly reviewed and revised, and urging compulsory rather than casual compliance.

Equal Opportunities Policy and Practice – Disability

This practical handbook by Elspeth Morrison is one of a series of booklets on areas of equal opportunity including race and gender, published by the Independent Theatre Council. Costing just £1, it contains ideas and information on how to include disabled people in the arts both as employees and in the audience. It briefly outlines their role within the arts from a historical and cultural perspective, dispelling the myth that disabled people are only recipients of art by discussing the emergence of a thriving disability arts movement, where work is created by, rather than for, disabled people, and because of, not in spite of, their experience of disability.

Although geared to theatre companies, the book would be useful reading for anyone working in the arts as an introduction to equal opportunities. While not intended as a definitive guide, it does provide broad guidelines on how to put policy into practice, explaining that this takes time, planning and commitment.

It suggests that venues should create their own workable targets, and monitor progress to ensure they are being met. It goes on to talk about the recruitment process, from advertising posts to interviewing and appointment, stressing that accurate targeting is essential to attract disabled employees since they often have a different information network to non-disabled people.

As regards publicity and audiences the book stresses disabled people should not only be targeted when disability is involved, but at all times, ensuring venues and performances are more accessible. It reminds readers of the potentially increased revenue through this largely untapped market. The guide also emphasises that all publicity, including that which goes into listings magazines, should contain basic access information, possibly in the form of the coding

---

[1] Social Policy Research Findings, no 21, 1991

[2] Published by Alf Morris MP, Shadow Minister for Disabled People's Rights

[3] Lord Rix, addressing Arts Council/Department of Employment seminar on Employment in the Arts for Disabled People, Brixton, 1992

system used by Artsline London (see page 51) giving details of full access, no access and partial access (where you are required to contact the venue for details).

Morrison explains the social barriers faced by disabled people, the difference between access, integration and discrimination – both direct and indirect, with examples of each. Environmental barriers and their possible solutions are discussed such as where to obtain money for adaptations, including the ADAPT Fund (see page 39).

A glossary of terms is given to explain such facilities as induction loops, minicom/vistel, sign language interpretation and audio description (where a trained person describes visual features of a performance). An appendix contains lists of useful organisations including specialist press, media and publications while examples of good practice are cited to encourage others to implement their own equal opportunities policy.

The book is not didactic, but explains the reasoning behind equal opportunities – an understanding of which is crucial if policies are to be implemented effectively since they require continued modification and genuine commitment.

Arts and Equality: Action Pack for Arts Organisations

Commissioned by the Arts Development Association in 1989, the action pack was researched and written by Christine Jackson, former head of research and policy at the Equal Opportunities Commission. Designed to help organisations devise and implement their own equal opportunities policies, it covers what a policy should contain, who it is for and who should be responsible for implementing and monitoring it. The pack also looks at forms of discrimination, and the constitution of management boards and advisory groups responsible for decision-making within an organisation. A section on marketing includes venue image, audience surveys and targeting. Another on recruitment covers advertising posts, staff training and interviews. It

also takes a brief look at aids such as induction loop systems and sign interpretation. Although concise, the pack acts as a useful starting point. It is not prescriptive, but advocates action, putting the onus on readers to follow through the guidelines and take on responsibility for adopting good policy.

The Fight to be Included: Black Disabled Perspectives in the Arts

This was the title of a one-day conference organised by the Minorities Arts Advisory Service (MAAS), a national black arts development agency. Held at the Black Art Gallery, north London, in October 1991 and funded by the Arts Council, it addressed the issues of double discrimination as experienced by black disabled people. The conference was intended as a reference point from which future policies and agendas for action could be developed. Its precursor was a two-day London conference, Race and Disability: A Dialogue for Action, held in June 1991 and organised by a steering group of black and Asian disabled people with support from the Greater London Association of Disabled People (GLAD). The first conference ever to address such issues, it involved both artists and art providers and looked at ways of ending discriminatory practice.

The Fight to be Included began with contributions from black disabled artists, including Peter McDonald, a poet and researcher; Nabil Shaban, actor and founder of GRAEAE Theatre Company; and Millie Hill, visual artist and co-founder of the Black Disabled People's Group. A slide presentation on American perspectives entitled "Art for Self-empowerment and Systematic Change" was given by Robert Harris, a visual artist and disabled activist, as part of his campaigning tour of the UK organised by the Arts Council.

Participants called for the right to be consulted about matters which affect their lives, to address gaps in service provision as users and service providers, and to represent themselves and create their own positive images to counter media stereotypes.

"Black disabled people are a minority within a minority to the point where they are virtually invisible. They are rejected and oppressed ...under-represented in all areas of society ...and discriminated against in areas of housing, education and employment."
Millie Hill

Photograph: Stephanie Henry, Format

The multiple discrimination experienced by black disabled women was also highlighted. Since there are no role models or positive images of them, the only portrayals perpetuate myths – the disabled woman as Superwoman, overcoming all odds; the "brilliant mind/crippled body", or the helpless victim to be pitied and treated in a "special" way.

Black disabled people feel isolated from their own culture through its lack of awareness and recognition of them. The emerging black disability movement is interested in forming alliances with other groups of disabled and non-disabled people in order to gain a position of collective strength from which to fight for their right to be included.

Museums and Galleries Disability Association (MAGDA)

Open to disabled and non-disabled people working in or with museum services, the aim of MAGDA is to achieve integration of disabled visitors and staff into museum services throughout the UK. MAGDA collects and disseminates information among museum professionals by means of seminars and publications, liaising between museum services and the various organisations representing disabled people.

Museums and Galleries Commission (MGC)

A code of practice on disability has been completed by Carolyn Keen, part-time disability adviser and former chair of MAGDA as part of the work undertaken by MGC in responding to the recommendations of the Attenborough Report,

Arts and Disabled People (1985), which looked at provision for disabled people in the arts. With funding assistance from the Carnegie (UK) Trust, Keen was appointed for a two-year period (subsequently extended to three years) to assess how MGC could support museums in providing opportunities for disabled people, both as visitors and employees.

The code applies to all museums, regardless of size, collection or funding. Each venue adopting the code will have to draw up a disability policy statement (DPS). In addition, an action plan — complete with time-table and budget to be co-ordinated by a designated senior member of staff and a staff working party — will be developed.

The DPS and action plan will be endorsed by the museum's governing body (which will have disabled representatives), published and made available to staff and contractors. Central to the code is the emphasis for each museum to establish a procedure for regular consultation with disabled people and disability outreach organisations.

Anti-discriminatory practice will be followed for recruitment, employment, training and promotion of disabled people (which extends to volunteers), with a system for monitoring and reviewing. As a first step, all staff will be given Disability Awareness Training, and personnel staff will receive equal opportunities employment training. All staff will be trained on how to facilitate access to the collections and services, following induction courses to ensure that they are aware of their responsibilities in fulfilling the spirit of DPS.

Other recommendations include exhibition, display and pricing policies, all taking account of the role of disabled people in society in a positive way. Community outreach programmes will be devised to introduce disabled people to a museum's facilities and to develop links with other agencies in the community, such as arts, leisure, education, social services, health and transport, in order to promote initiatives that will benefit disabled people.

All publicity, information and advertisements

will be presented in a variety of forms, giving details helpful to disabled people, i.e. transport and parking facilities, and these will be verified by disabled people as part of the continuing procedure of consultation.

Ikon, Birmingham

The Ikon Gallery was set up 25 years ago by Birmingham artists and has grown from a small-scale enterprise to a major gallery for contemporary art. Funded by the Arts Council, West Midlands Arts and the City Council, it attracts over 1,000 visitors a week.

The gallery implements a comprehensive equal opportunities policy, with phased, targeted objectives which have been drawn up between local disability organisations and its own council of management. For all advertised posts, the number of disabled applicants is monitored by means of questionnaires to ensure appropriate and effective targeting and publicity. Recent access improvements to the gallery include modification of the information desk to a wheelchair-accessible height, and the provision of tape guides for exhibitions and gallery orientation.

As part of its programming policy, Ikon tries to maintain equal opportunities by taking exhibitions out to people in hospitals and day centres. It has included work by disabled artists in a number of in-house exhibitions. Johnnie Gathercole, who works collaboratively with his sister Maggie (see page 20), was one of seven featured artists in *Human Properties* (January–February 1992), an exhibition which looked at artists' responses to buildings and environments that are significant to them.

Artlink West Yorkshire (formerly Shape Up North)

Artlink West Yorkshire, an arts agency based in Leeds, creates access to the arts with disabled people through workshops, touring performances, exhibitions of their work in mainstream galleries, and courses on Disability Awareness and Equality Training. It receives funding from Yorkshire and Humberside Arts Board, West Yorkshire Grants, district health authorities, social and leisure services, trusts, businesses and donations.

Over 50 per cent of its workforce are disabled or have particular needs, and a disability support fund has recently been established to pay for equipment and training for new employees. Andrea Lamb, who is visually impaired, has run the organisation's ticket scheme since 1987 (see page 55). Her appointment was one of positive discrimination to help the project become self-running by disabled members and their volunteers. Lamb has created an administration system which combines braille, tactile relief and audio information, to enable both non-sighted and sighted staff to pick up each other's work. She uses a talking typewriter for correspondence, a tape recorder for messages and stencils for making bookings and receipts.

She is also one of three Disability Awareness Trainers at Artlink, and receives training in this and in other areas of work. Assisted by two volunteer workers, she remains in control, being, as she says, "supported rather than patronised".

Lamb gives presentations at day centres to help promote the ticket scheme and other Artlink services. As a disabled person, she helps raise public awareness by demonstrating that disabled people can be the facilitators.

Johnnie Gathercole from *Beyond the Barriers*. Photograph: J & M Gathercole

the road to enlightenment

"A chain is only as strong as its weakest link."

"It takes one frontline member of staff without disability awareness only a matter of seconds to negate the effort and investment made by colleagues and management. If Disability Awareness Training is to be effective it must be run on a continuing basis, especially where staff turnover is high."
Disabled Living Foundation

Disability Awareness and Equality Training is one of the most fundamental means of effecting change in venues. Anti-discrimination legislation on its own is not enough. Changes in attitude, understanding and awareness have to occur on a personal level before they can be made on a professional one. Training is not didactic, but carried out in consultation with professional disabled trainers, in a relaxed, unjudgemental way, where fears and prejudices can be discussed and dispelled to reach a clearer understanding of disabled people's needs.

Shape London Training
Shape London has established itself as a key provider of consultancy and advice on Disability Awareness Training (DAT) within the arts, setting up courses for clients, including Battersea Arts Centre and Sadlers Wells Theatre, and carrying out extensive research into resources, tutor training and support.

In 1990, it secured a major project grant from the Arts Council to develop DAT work over the year. This included taking DAT into large arts venues, and organising a three-day course for disabled actors from the GRAEAE Theatre in Education Company to enable them to incorporate DAT in their performance and workshop tours to schools.

Shape London Training continues to respond to a massive demand for DAT from staff and management committees of arts organisations in London as a result of increased awareness, created in part by the work of organisations like Shape. One of its courses, More Than Just a Ticket, was targeted at front-of-house staff in major venues participating in the Shape Ticket Scheme (see page 55). Led by disabled trainers, the course reviewed current access, safety regulations, customer services and other issues relating to disabled audiences.

Deaf and blind trainer leading a workshop in working with visually impaired people. Photograph: Sally Lancaster, Photof

another school of thought

Historically there has been a lack of access to arts education for disabled adults. Some mainstream colleges are at last widening their doors, offering improved facilities such as specialised equipment, note-takers and sign interpreters. Several colleges of education for disabled people, such as the Royal National College for the Blind, Hereford, and the National Star Centre, Cheltenham, have established their own art departments and studios, allowing students to study art to a professional standard, often working in collaboration with other art colleges and practising artists, and widely exhibiting work.

Arts Management Centre, University of Northumbria at Newcastle

The centre offers a short-course programme to arts managers, trainees, administrators and volunteers on all aspects of arts management. All courses are held at locations which are accessible by public transport and wheelchair-user friendly. The centre also offers signers, note-takers and assistance with travel.

It sets up training courses for arts organisations to establish and implement equal opportunities policy and practice. With the assistance of Equal Arts (see page 77), Shape Training (see page 78), and Right Track Training (a consortium of Disability Equality Trainers) a pilot two-day course was held in 1991 to examine practical ways of achieving equal access.

Hereward College, Coventry

This college for disabled students provides an integrated learning environment where emphasis is on empowerment. The college runs an arts foundation course, from which over 80 per cent of students go on to study at degree level. Students benefit from having a self-study centre which is tutor supported at all times, and open 12 hours a day, seven days a week, and from the close links the college maintains with Coventry University where students work on day release.

Creative Arts Department, National Star Centre College of Further Education, Cheltenham

Opened in 1991, the department offers disabled students access to a purpose-built design and photographic studio, darkroom, 3D sculpture workshop, theatre and theatre studios. By exposing

Student of National Star Centre creating a sculpture in the Forest of Dean. Photograph: Arts Access

Right: Students working at The Wildfowl Trust, Slimbridge, weaving pollarded willows to construct a flamingo. Photograph: Julian Davies

students to a wide range of experience, the department seeks to promote independence, professional practice and encourage self-esteem. It also offers the opportunity to study for recognised qualifications, such as the City and Guilds certificate in photography, the BTEC first diploma in design and leisure, and an arts foundation course.

Sculpture students have worked with a professional sculptor on location for a week on the Forest of Dean sculpture trail. With the help of the Forestry Commission students could easily access the forest. After a day spent exploring the trail, the students created their own sculptures, working alongside artist Gary Fabian-Miller. One series was entitled *The Lizard, the Bird and the Pit*. This comprised a 30-foot lizard made from branches and grass which wove its way through the trees before descending into a pit of spiralling stones.

A second group explored the concept of night and day in the forest. A deer made from a root stump, branches and dried leaves "slept" under a sun of yellow leaves pinned into the earth by fine twigs. The surrounding ground was scraped

bare to reveal the dark earth, reflecting night, along with shooting stars of stones and acorns. The students later shared their experience with local adult occupation centre members in a weekend workshop.

The department brings in visiting artists to run life classes, workshops and projects in painting, drawing, ceramics and illustration. Students have collaborated with London's Royal Court and Everyman theatres in workshops at the college's theatre. The theatre has also hosted numerous performances by companies such as the Royal Shakespeare Company, the Royal Academy of Music and GRAEAE Theatre Company.

To enhance the arts experience, students regularly visit exhibitions nationally and abroad, and have the opportunity to work on placements in local business. "The Creative Arts Department is constantly developing, widening the scope of experience in the arts for students who have the interest to explore within a professional environment exciting opportunities awaiting them in the creative field," explains David Finch, Head of Creative Arts.

a lift to the top

With lack of access to vocational training, disabled people have low levels of expectation. Opportunities are, however, gradually opening up, with the creation of training schemes geared to meet disabled people's needs.

Arts Management Traineeship, Equal Arts, Gateshead

Equal Arts established an arts management traineeship — the north-east region's first — in recognition of the lack of opportunities for disabled people in the arts and specifically to gain the training or work experience necessary to secure employment in arts management.

Funded by the Arts Council, Tyne and Wear Foundation and Charity Projects for an initial 15-month period, and managed and overseen by Equal Arts, the traineeship consisted of two placements, each of five months, based at major arts organisations in Newcastle. Recruitment was targeted locally, regionally and nationally, through the disability press and employment organisations.

The traineeship went to Kirin Saeed, a visually impaired woman with a Higher National Diploma in public administration. It was her first real employment opportunity. The traineeship covered all aspects of arts administration, including communication, fundraising, financial management, marketing and recruitment. It also offered in-house training experience at the two fully accessible venues, complemented by short courses at the University of Northumbria at Newcastle Arts Management Centre and elsewhere. A salary of £8,175 was paid to cover training costs, travel and out-of-pocket expenses.

Saeed had specific practical needs, and the Disability Advisory Service supplied a range of equipment along with training. This included a personal computer and printer, a voice synthesizer and a braille jotter (a small portable computer for taking notes). They also arranged transport to and from work, and to meetings.

A support group was formed comprising four women, two of whom were disabled. This group included Maggie Goodbarn of AIRS (see page 50)

and Frances Fairman, short-course leader of the Arts Management Centre, University of Northumbria at Newcastle. They met Saeed on a regular basis to discuss progress, give moral support and iron out any problems.

The traineeship commenced in July 1990 with the first placement at Projects UK, a production-based multi-media arts organisation. Pre-placement preparation included Disability Equality Training for all staff. Saeed's timetable, although full-time, was flexible to allow a day a week for background reading and documentation.

During the placement, Saeed completed two projects, including a drama and photography project run by and for disabled people looking at representation of disability by the media, and exploring self-image. The second placement, at Northern Arts, began in January 1991 with an induction period into arts funding. Here, Saeed undertook a research project, monitoring the arts and disability work of the region's Local Arts Development Agencies (LADAs) which resulted in a written report and recommendations.

The latter part of the traineeship involved Saeed in a three-month research project based at University of Northumbria at Newcastle which looked at the feasibility of multiple arts management traineeships, including two-year placements and accreditation. Funded by The Chase Charity, the research gave Saeed the opportunity to evaluate her own training experience, and look at ways of modifying and improving it for future trainees.

Following this study, which was published as a report, Saeed began a nine-month supported work placement at Tyneside Cinema, an independent film theatre in Newcastle. Funded by the British Film Institute and the Arts Council, this work extended Saeed's traineeship to two years.

The arts management traineeship was a pilot scheme for the region which aimed not only to provide a significant and structured training opportunity in the arts for one disabled person, but also to establish a model which could be replicated

"One of the most positive aspects of the traineeship was that I earned a wage. This was important to me, for it made me feel part of society. Taking notice of my suggestions made me feel stronger and more independent." Kirin Saeed. Photograph: Pete Fryer

by other arts organisations. It was designed to influence future employment practices and improve staff profiles in the region, as well as increase opportunities for disabled people in the arts, and demonstrate to them that employment in the field is both a viable and interesting option.

Traineeship Programme, The Mix, London

The Mix is a group of community arts facilitators based in Finchley, north London. It is funded by Barnet Council, the London Arts Board, Trust for London, the Baring Foundation and the Milly Apthorp Trust. Established in 1987, with the aim of integrating people with learning difficulties into the local community through mixed-media artwork, it has national significance through its progressive work but retains a local relevance.

In 1990, it started up a two-year traineeship programme, giving three people the opportunity to learn how to run community arts workshops by working alongside trained artists. Recruitment was initially through advertisements in the specialist press and direct approach to day centres, colleges and homes in surrounding boroughs. The trainees

piloted the project themselves, constantly evaluating and modifying the programme to suit their needs, in line with The Mix's philosophy of self-advocacy. The long-term aim is that trainees will become permanent workers for The Mix.

Shape London Training Programme

Since 1985, Shape London has organised a training programme under the auspices of training officer Keith Pickard. This has included training for artists and health and social services staff, and vocational training and training placements for disabled people. Shape has also organised skills training in stage lighting, photography and interview techniques in response to a request from people with learning difficulties from the Camden People First self-advocacy group and the Heart 'n' Soul performance group.

One of its most ambitious undertakings was the initiation of three year-long, full-time arts management training placements for disabled people. Run consecutively at Battersea Arts Centre, the Leicester Haymarket and the Whitechapel Art Gallery, Michael Turner now works as head of information and technology for the Greater London Association of Disabled People; Penny Hefferan was appointed music officer at East Midlands Arts; and I have been working as an arts and disability consultant since leaving the Whitechapel Art Gallery, London.

Shape also established a three-month training placement for a visually impaired community artist with a performing theatre company, set up six apprenticeship placements for disabled artists to work alongside art tutors to learn workshop skills, and initiated two traineeships for young deaf actors at the Unicorn Theatre to develop tutoring skills for working with children.

Shape recently embarked on a major training and employment initiative, Shape Into Work, which provides a structured programme of training and work placements for young disabled people wishing to pursue careers within the arts as performers, technicians, tutors or managers.

Whitechapel Art Gallery, London

6 changing landscapes

art in the open

Ceramic and Wooden Birds, Ayr, by adults with learning difficulties, Project Ability, 1990. Photograph: Neil McLeod

Very few opportunities have arisen in the public art sector for disabled artists in the past. Slowly the situation is improving, as increasing numbers of public art commissioning agencies and authorities take on board the meaning of equal opportunities. Yet since artists have traditionally used foundries or fabricators to produce large artworks, it is often only when on-site work is executed that extra support may be required.

Public art provides an excellent means of changing public attitudes, because artists become highly visible in the process, either from being on site or through high-profile publicity. The Public Art Forum — the national association that promotes and advances high professional standards for public art practice in this country — has recently revised its constitution to encourage equality of opportunity and to ensure "public" (and that includes disabled people) access to future commissioned work.

Art In the Open – Raku Works, Sculptural Arts

Based in Accrington, Lancashire, Raku Works is a registered charity and limited company. Set up in 1984, it organises sculpture projects run by professional artists specialising in ceramics within educational and community venues. The overall aim is to increase access to arts activity.

Raku Works is staffed by two project workers, two administrators and an artistic director, supported by a pool of freelance artists. It undertakes large-scale works with individual groups, sometimes collaborating with other community organisations, using themes and practices which reflect the community and environment.

Working in a flexible way, Raku designs projects to meet the needs of groups, priority being given to under-resourced groups and those traditionally not involved in arts activity. The company has established a reputation for being innovative and for widening the educational experience of crafts for a cross-section of people.

In the early days, projects varied from short, experimental raku glaze-firings (based on Japanese pottery techniques), to large-scale community commissions. Now, however, the company concentrates upon the latter, since these have a longer-lasting effect on participants. The work aims to promote personal growth and creative thinking,

The Cuerdan Valley Park Project was a collaboration between Raku Works, the Lancashire Trust for Nature Conservancy and community groups

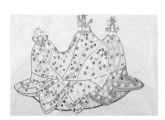

The Colour Design for the Cuerdan Valley Park Project by adults with learning difficulties from Lisieux Hall, Chorley. Photographs: Paul Goodwin

thereby enriching the lives of individuals and their communities.

In recent years, the company has worked with secondary, junior and disabled children's schools to give children unique opportunities outside their usual school experience. Artists guide them through an intensive, creative process, which involves the design and construction of ceramic sculptures. Through this process they acquire technical skills and an understanding of and confidence in their own creative ability.

Raku has run several mosaic projects whereby groups collaborate on designs drawn from their own cultures, identities and communities. Experience has proved mosaic-making to be ideal for group projects because the process of moving from two dimensions to three, from design to construction, is straightforward yet challenging, while the product is visually exciting and represents the concerns and interests of its creators.

Having worked as artists-in-residence from its inception, Raku Works is aware that successful projects rely on the understanding and co-operation of all involved. This is achieved through in-service training, which encourages teachers to take advantage of the artists' presence, and gives them an idea of the working methods employed. It believes that through understanding, staff are better placed to share in the project and continue the work when the residency ends. Training involves a presentation of Raku's work, and short courses in which participants are taken through a condensed version of the longer project.

The Self-Image project lasted five weeks and was based at Moss Lea day centre, Ormskirk, Lancashire, in early 1991. Three artists and a musician working with staff and centre users transformed a room into a stunning visual and audio environment based on the theme of self-image. Funded by Lancashire Social Services, Lancashire County Council, Merseyside Arts, West Lancashire District Council, North West Shape and Marks and Spencer, the aim was to aid the transition of centre users back into the community.

Dragon Seat, **Green End Infant School, by START OUT. Photograph: Sameena Hussein, SNAPS**

Centre users learnt techniques such as design and self-expression through painting. Ideas which reflected individual identity, aspiration and achievement were then transferred into clay and papier mâché, producing large sculptural forms. Music workshops on the same theme were organised and recordings were made, from which a score was elicited and transposed into a visual artwork.

Another project involved Raku being commissioned by CREATE, a hospital-based arts organisation, to work with people with learning difficulties at the Royal Albert Hospital in Lancaster. The long-stay hospital is scheduled to be closed, with residents moving back into the community. The hospital authorities wanted to mark this transition with a permanent public artwork. With a budget of £10,000, a quarter of which came from the hospital itself, Raku Works ran workshops for residents over a six-week period. The result was a wheelchair user-friendly sculptural seat reflecting the participants' view of the world, sited in Williamson Park, one of Lancaster's most popular public places.

START OUT

START OUT produces environmental artworks and was developed out of START Studio (see page 36). Funded by the Manchester/Salford Inner Cities Programme and co-ordinated by two part-time artists, it aims to increase employment opportunities for START members and associate artists. The main thrust of START OUT's work is production of environmental artwork involving local communities,

> *"Experience has proved mosaic-making to be ideal for group projects because the process of moving from two dimensions to three, from design to construction, is straightforward yet challenging, while the product is visually exciting and represents the concerns and interests of its creators."*
> Raku Works

usually outside the health service. START OUT works in a variety of media including mosaic, textiles and wood, drawing on the skills and resources available at the studio. The first major project was a collaboration with the Community Technical Aid Centre which produced *Dragon Seat*, a large sculptural bench. The project involved over 200 people and took six months to complete. Sited in the playground of Green End Infant School, Burnage, Manchester, *Dragon Seat* serves two purposes — it improves the unprepossessing school front while providing seating for parents waiting to collect their children.

Other projects have included working at Booth Hall Children's Hospital, north Manchester, where START OUT was commissioned by Lancashire Wildlife Trust to create a mosaic archway for a wildlife garden, working with patients from the hospital. In association with the Community Aid Centre, START OUT has also worked with teachers and children of St Ambrose Primary School in Manchester to design and create a painted timber fence for the school, incorporating images of trees, flowers and animals.

Echo City

Echo City is a London-based band of musician-designers formed in 1983 with the aim of turning musical instruments into permanent outdoor play structures or "sonic playgrounds". It runs projects with disabled and non-disabled people, combining music and the visual arts, designing and building permanent installations, and creating new environments. Echo City also operates a mobile sonic playground, taking the concept into a wide range of settings for short-term projects and public performances, thereby involving a cross-section of the community in the creative process of making music and art.

Past projects include work for the Glasgow Garden Festival, tours of psychiatric hospitals and community centres in the north of England, and major performance events around the world. Instruments include *Bell Tower*, a triangular

Formerly a hairdresser's shop, the house in the Avenues — an area of urban regeneration — was transformed into a temporary site-specific gallery.

Patio doors by members of Whinney House Resource Centre. Photograph: Keith Alexander

structure built of aluminium scaffolding from which hang *Oxibells*, prepared gas cylinders that can be played with a nylon clapper, and *Shimmer*, a 15-metre-wide sculpture comprising tuned lengths of aluminium bar suspended from parallel stainless steel cables, its notes being activated by rope bell-pull or the wind.

Avenues House Project, Gateshead

June 1991 saw the end of a two-year project involving Gateshead artist-in-residence Keith Alexander and over 500 local people in the creation of arts and crafts work for the decoration of a house. Formerly a hairdresser's shop, the house in the Avenues — an area of urban regeneration — was transformed into a temporary site-specific gallery.

Alexander had previously made *A Room for Gateshead* for the Tyne International exhibition at the National Garden Festival in 1990. Using the concept of making an artistic statement out of everyday domestic objects and pieces of furniture, it provided a taster for this larger project on the same theme.

The Avenues House Project was directed by Alexander and co-ordinated by Gateshead Libraries and Arts as part of its public arts programme. It was the biggest single community-based arts project the latter had ever funded. Additional support and financial assistance was provided by Gateshead planning, social services and education departments, and Tyne International. The end-of-terrace house in Brinkburn Avenue was leased free of charge by Northern Rock Housing Trust.

Before the project commenced, local residents were leafleted and two meetings were convened to introduce the idea of the project, elicit responses and stimulate support. It was always the intention that it should be a "living project", both in terms of local involvement, and in being an enduring statement about home living space and the lives of its inhabitants.

Alexander was already working closely with community groups as part of his residency, and for this project he worked with disabled people, adults with learning difficulties, women's groups and pupils from six schools, among them one for children with behavioural problems. In addition, an Employment Training placement — a wood carver/welder — worked alongside Alexander for the last year of the project.

Alexander believes that increasing people's understanding of the concerns and processes of practising artists helps them develop their own artistic skills. On the house project he helped people convert their ideas into finished items for the house without losing the original vitality. Workshops in stained-glass window, print and mosaic making were held at Avenues House. These were complemented by visits by participants to various local industries to observe how objects such as plaster ceiling roses and ceramic tiles were made. These methods were then adopted for their own work, but with freer application. Once a month, "open" workshops were held to enable and encourage residents from the Avenues area to become involved. These also served to generate support and publicity. Out of the "closed" workshops (those involving community groups) emerged over 40 pieces of arts and crafts work, all

on the theme of domesticity and each illustrating a tale of its manufacture or of its maker's view of family and community life.

The first artwork a visitor to the house encounters is the front garden mosaic. Created by people with learning difficulties from Whinney House Resource Centre, Gateshead, it depicts their view of the environment. To the rear of the house is a "fantasy yard" mosaic depicting a bed on a desert island, by Bensham Grove Women's Group. The bed, complete with headboard, was designed by Alexander and contains real flowers. A pastoral note is introduced by wooden carved sheep on the front porch, a statement about Gateshead's pre-industrial roots. The door itself depicts the process of its carving and forms an appropriate introduction to the project.

Stained-glass windows made by Bensham Grove Women's Group and disabled adults from Fountainview Day Centre, with assistance from professional artist/glass makers, provide a colourful backdrop against which the indoor drama is staged. Alexander's work in particular involves the telling of stories and setting of scenes through art. The bedroom walls, for instance, are festooned with images of sleep, from silent slumbers and dreams through to noisy nightmares.

In the sitting-room, net curtains created by people with learning difficulties from New Road Adult Training Centre are hung with images suggesting the fragility between that which lies outside and that which is kept inside.

A sofa cover designed and printed by adults from Whinney House, Fountainview Day Centre and St Chad's Community Group is scattered with images from television. And the ceiling rose, made by 11- to 14-year-olds from Furrowfield Special School, is an inverted tea-table strewn with plates of plaster baked beans, Yorkshire pudding and parsnips.

In the bathroom, surreal ceramic tiling reflects a shower scene. The lino matting underfoot has been spray-stencilled with pictures of bathroom floor clutter, discarded socks and underwear, soap

It was always the intention that it should be a "living project", both in terms of local involvement, and in being an enduring statement about home living space and the lives of its inhabitants.

Ceiling rose by pupils of Furrowfield Special School. Photograph: Allan Glenwright

Right: David and Doris from
Whinney House Resource Centre
beside the tiled hearth which
reflects the joy of getting home
after being out in bad weather.
Photograph: Powerhouse
Photography

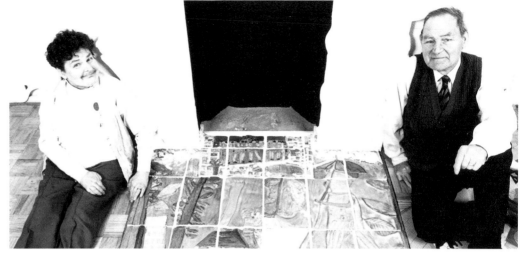

and shampoo bottles. Here a women's group has taken the theme of bathroom chaos into the framework of a stained-glass window, where it reflects the domestic harmony and discord which dominates everyday life.

Avenues House was open as a "showcase for the arts" for public viewing between June and August and again, due to popular demand, throughout October, 1991. The ground floor of the house was wheelchair accessible, with widened doors and ramps. Personal guided tours were provided for visitors and information boards giving further details were displayed around the house.

The catalogue for this exhibition was totally in keeping with the theme of the project. In the form of an estate agent's specifications for prospective house buyers it gave details such as rooms and features, and information on how to get there and viewing times.

When the temporary residents, the artworkers, moved out of this "alternative Ideal Home" they were able to remove their artifacts for their own use and public display, thus fulfilling the spirit of community ownership.

Avenues House has been heralded as an exemplar of good practice in both public and community art, where good intentions have been more than matched by the results. In recognition of its achievements Gateshead Libraries and Arts won the Northern Electric/Tyne Tees Award for Visual Arts, and Keith Alexander was runner-up in the

Environmental Art category. In 1992, Gateshead Libraries and Arts was also runner-up for the annual Prudential Award for excellence in the arts for the second year running (the only local authority to reach the visual arts finals), where the Avenues project was specifically mentioned. With the Northern Region, which encompasses Tyne and Wear, having won the bid to be the Arts Council's "City of Culture" in 1996, Gateshead Libraries and Arts are considering a similar project in the future, thereby bringing it into the wider arena.

Carousel, Creative Arts By and With People With Learning Difficulties, Brighton

Carousel promotes the active participation of people with learning difficulties in the arts through organising workshops, residencies, performances and exhibitions. Led by a team of four arts practitioners, an administrator-cum-development worker with additional contracted-in help, it engages a large number of volunteer artists.

Carousel relies on financial assistance from the Arts Council, South East Arts, Hove and Brighton Borough Councils, East Sussex Social Services and Brighton Health Authority. Additional support is received from trusts, businesses and the local community.

Participatory workshops form the main body of Carousel's work, ranging from one day to

The Living Environment,
Connaught Theatre (1991).
Photograph: Carousel

several months in length. Held in day centres, hospitals and schools, they cover music, visual art, drama, dance and movement, often in combination, and provide multi-sensory stimulation to encourage people to formulate creative ideas. These workshops also provide a supportive and consistent environment which enables individuals to develop their confidence and take more risks in extending their self-expression. They give opportunity for working in groups, while allowing everyone to take part at their own level and pace.

Much of Carousel's work focuses on the process of creativity rather than the finished product. However, Carousel believes there is significant value in making visible the work of artists with learning difficulties, particularly in mainstream venues from which they are normally excluded. Thus much of its work leads directly to public performance and exhibition.

"It is important that people with learning difficulties are taking an active part in the artistic and cultural life of the community, and public presentation of the work not only gives a sense of satisfaction and achievement to those directly involved but helps challenge prejudice and assumptions about the contribution disabled people can make to the arts," says one Carousel worker.

Carousel has a regular performance group comprising 10 people with learning difficulties from the Brighton and Hove area, and four Carousel project workers. The group meets throughout the year to rehearse, perform and explore new ideas. In 1990, a three-year artistic skill and development programme was started to promote self-advocacy within the group. This programme includes seeing performance work by other companies, and developing decision-making abilities in order that members might lead or co-lead future Carousel workshops.

Training is an integral part of Carousel's work through which volunteer artists, staff and participants are able to develop their artistic and communication skills. Based on practical arts work it includes exploration of issues and attitudes around disability and non-verbal communication,

and is supported by regular evaluation. Carousel is also committed to organising training for staff in education, social and health services, as well as for community artists and professional performers. Another facet of Carousel's work is residency projects. In February 1991, a two-week project took place at the Conaught Theatre, Worthing. Two Carousel workers collaborated with Liz Whitehead, a Brighton-based visual artist, to work with local people from three day centres. Centred on movement, music and visual art, the project resulted in an exhibition entitled *The Living Environment*.

This transformed the Conaught's Ritz Ballroom into a "designer house for sale". A series of rooms included a dream-filled bedroom with vertical bed complete with sleeping performers; an out-size kitchen with human taps and a five-foot-tall cheese-grater; a living room with "living" portraits; and a musical garden containing a life-size vegetable patch. The "house" was open to the public over two days as a walk-through exhibition.

Castle Park Project, Bristol

In May 1992, a 13-acre designated "green area" in the centre of Bristol became the site for a new environmental art project. A team of archæologists, landscape architects, artists and craftspeople have worked collaboratively with Bristol City Council Leisure Services Directorate to "put the heart back into the city", using open space rather than buildings.

Lesley Greene, former director and founder of the Public Art Development Trust, commissioned artworks which will both enhance the landscape and aid historical understanding of the site where Bristol essentially began. Points of interest are marked by interpretation panels and the Parks Department has prepared an audio guide to the area. Braille plaques mark each commissioned artwork while blind poet Dennis Casling's poetic texts have been inscribed into stone with the help of a calligrapher, offering a creative interpretation of the history of the site.

"It is important that people with learning difficulties are taking an active part in the artistic and cultural life of the community."
Carousel

trailblazers

Yorkshire Sculpture Park and Grizedale Forest have both developed "access trails" in response to the growing number of disabled visitors wishing to enjoy art in the open air and in recognition of the inaccessibility of the terrain of existing areas.

One area where there has been a lot of progress vis-à-vis public art and disabled people is in the development of sculpture trails. In the Forest of Dean, a four-mile trail has been made accessible by the Forestry Commission. River gullies have been filled, paths levelled and stiles replaced by swing gates, in response to disabled students from the National Star Centre, Cheltenham (see page 75) and Arts Access who have worked on their own sculpture projects within the forest over the past few years. Yorkshire Sculpture Park and Grizedale Forest have both developed "access trails" in response to the growing number of disabled visitors wishing to enjoy art in the open air and in recognition of the inaccessibility of the terrain of existing areas.

Grizedale Forest Access Trail

The Theatre in the Forest, a charitable trust established in 1969 by former forester Bill Grant, was the first public recreational scheme for the Forestry Commission. Located in the 9,000-acre Grizedale Forest between Lake Windermere and Coniston Water in Cumbria, the site now houses one of the country's largest collections of

Arched entrance by Jim Partridge. Photograph: Dick Capel

environmental sculpture.

As director of the project, Grant has spearheaded development of the arts programme at Grizedale since it began and facilities now include a 225-seat accessible theatre for dance, music and drama, a 9.5-mile sculpture trail, with approximately 68 works, a gallery showing working drawings and maquettes serving as an introduction to the open-air sculpture, a workshop for woodcraft and a studio for painting residencies.

Grizedale has a strong policy of supporting new artists, and has developed strong international links, hosting artists from America, Europe and Japan through residencies. Operating with a small core of staff, it relies on a large body of voluntary support. It receives about 200,000 visitors per year and has a commitment to making the arts both an educational and an enjoyable experience for all ages and abilities. Grizedale has won several awards in recognition of its achievements including the English Tourist Board Tourist Enterprise Award (1971 and 1972), Arts in Offices Award for art in a working environment (1986), the Northern Electric Arts Award to the director (1989) and the Prudential Arts Award (1990).

The Theatre in the Forest prioritises access and has had a lift, induction loop and adapted toilets installed in the theatre. The gallery and crafts workshop were made fully accessible when converted from an old saw mill, with good parking facilities to the whole site. There is a nature "touch trail" in the forest with rope guides, for the benefit of young, elderly and partially sighted visitors.

Assisted by funds from Northern Arts and South Lakeland District Council, the Theatre in the Forest has been developing a sculpture trail which is accessible to disabled people and others unable to use the existing long-distance trail. The new trail is in two sections divided by a natural ravine. This is bridged by a sculptural high-level walkway, to provide the challenging experience of moving through the tree tops. Artworks specific to the site and to the nature of the trail, including "touch" and "sound" pieces, have been incorporated into

Access sculpture trail, YSP, showing the "village" with tree house. Photograph: Albert Booth

the forest landscape. There are also resting places and passing points at regular intervals. A foot rail runs along the entire length of the trail to act as a visual and tactile guide in addition to clear signposting.

The trail has been developed over several years and the first section is now complete, with the remainder to be completed by the end of 1992.

Yorkshire Sculpture Park (YSP)

The Yorkshire Sculpture Park lies approximately six miles from Wakefield where it attracts many visitors from all over Britain and abroad. Set in 80 acres of landscaped parkland, it provides a setting for exhibitions, permanently sited sculptures and works on loan.

Founded as a charitable trust in 1977 by Peter Murray, executive director, it is essentially a "gallery without walls". Being easily accessible by road and rail, and with busy education and community programmes involving workshops and residencies, the public can enjoy and learn about sculpture in the open air and see artists at work. Funding comes principally from Yorkshire and

Humberside Arts Board, Wakefield Metropolitan District Council, West Yorkshire Grants and the Henry Moore Foundation.

The policy of the park has always been to encourage the public to touch the exhibits, considering the tactile experience vital to the understanding and appreciation of sculpture. As such, it attracts many disabled people, many preferring or requiring to explore sculpture in this way, although the terrain and scale of the landscape makes access difficult even when using the electric "Booster Scooters" provided.

The park is open daily and has free admission and parking. A shop and information centre adjacent to the car park are accessible to wheelchair users, and adapted toilet facilities are located nearby, with more in the café and along the new access sculpture trail.

This trail, completed in 1991, was developed from the trust's commitment to make sculpture accessible to everyone, particularly disabled people. The project has turned one area of the park into a trail which combines sculpture and nature, providing a multi-sensory experience. British sculptor Don

Herb garden. Photograph: YSP

Rankin was commissioned to design and manage the trail, working closely with other artists, craftspeople, landscape designers and disabled people. He was supported in varying degrees by the Community Project, Employment Training Scheme, craftspeople, students and many volunteers.

The trail, which occupies five acres, was inspired by "the grand spiral". This can be observed in all aspects of the work, from the use of water, grass, trees and shrubs to the serpentine movement of the pathways. Built in two stages it required careful planning and consultation with future users to avoid the creation of something tokenistic. Everyone understood that the result could not be perfect first time around, therefore a theme which would provide a sense of growth and evolution, while having the potential for long-term change, was adopted.

Phase one, which involved major formal landscaping, features site-specific sculptures, many reminiscent of 18th-century follies, drawing inspiration from the Bretton estate on which the park lies. The *Moving Road* by Rankin, a pathway of hexagonal blocks, off-cuts from the wooden pagoda sited at the trail entrance, provides underfoot visual excitement with gradually changing patterns. Other paths, all with a gentle gradient and made from materials which remain dry and non-slip, wind around the trail, with frequent rest areas and wide passing points. Banked by rare grasses, flowers and plants, the pathways provide contrasts of colour, tone and texture. Overlapping the paths these "hedgerows" provide a visual feast at wheelchair-accessible height, and can be brushed against, releasing their scent.

A "ruined village" lies at the centre of the trail, which incorporates a wooden tree-house, picnic area with tables and seating, and even a phone box folly. In its "garden" is a dead tree that has been transformed into a sculptural spectacle by Rankin, its vast root system echoed in slate. A disabled person's toilet, funded by Wakefield Metropolitan District Council's equal opportunities unit, appropriately takes on the appearance of a ruined building.

A nearby well contains seven steel fish swimming around in its depths. The theme of water continues outside the "village" with a miniature aqueduct and a water garden complete with a bridge, which has been carved from a single tree trunk. Water cascades down from surrounding slopes into streams running alongside the paths, providing contrasts of sound. These are echoed by tree and shrub movement.

Phase two, which was completed in the summer of 1991, constituted landscaping of a more natural kind. Here the trail meanders through yew trees and bushes, creating a "secret space" in contrast to the open space of phase one. A hidden mosaic is revealed as leaves are brushed aside. There are other surprises such as sculptures peering out from the undergrowth or from within a cluster of rhododendron bushes.

Benches carved from fallen trees and others sculpted by artists provide resting places from which to take in the smells and sounds of nature and catch musical chimes jangling in the wind. There are also regular vantage points and, at the far end of the trail, a restored Victorian arbour provides a vista of the whole park.

The creation of the trail did not involve imposing an idea or a single vision on the landscape, but rather emerged organically and through continued consultation with disabled people. Advisers from Artlink West Yorkshire (see page 73) and Wakefield Access Unit played an important role in the trail's ultimate success, as did the many disabled people who came to try it out at various stages. In addition, all of the 20 staff of the sculpture park were involved in its development and received Disability Awareness Training prior to the start of the project and at various intervals thereafter.

Hickson International plc, Yorkshire Arts Association, the Gulbenkian Foundation, UK 2000 and the Business Sponsorship Incentive Scheme provided the main funding for the trail, the total cost of which amounted to approximately £250,000.

Money-in-kind was given from numerous other companies. The Yorkshire Sculpture Park won the 1988 ABSA Award for Best Sponsorship of the Arts with disabled people. The trail attracts many visitors, and an information leaflet in large print and in braille has been produced to ensure people know what is available. It is also a valuable educational resource used by numerous schools and centres. The park's education programme already involves working with disabled children through workshops using natural, bio-degradable materials found in the park, and "touch" exhibitions.

The appointment of a community arts officer, funded by the Carnegie (UK) Trust over two years, has allowed interpretive and community activities based around the trail to be extended, with particular emphasis on disabled people.

Well with Fish sculpture by Brian Fell

... and in health

Included here are some examples of hospital art projects which have involved disabled artists as positive role models – that is, not as patients, but as professionals working in healthcare settings — a growth area in the field of public art.

Hammersmith Hospital Disabled Artist-in-Residence Project

The art committee of Hammersmith Hospital, which has an extensive and expanding art collection, decided in 1990 to host their first arts-residency with the purpose of creating a site-specific work for permanent display at the busy teaching hospital. It was felt that a disabled artist would bring more to the residency, providing a useful role model of the disabled person as the professional rather than the patient, while also furthering his or her own career. The need for a flexible and supportive framework was identified.

Christine Ross, public art officer for the Borough of Hammersmith and Fulham, took on the role of overseer to liaise between the art committee, the artist and other parties involved. The Public Art Development Trust, which had advised the art committee for several years, agreed to help manage and fundraise, while British Health Care Arts took on the task of monitoring and documenting the project.

Funding for the residency was provided by Opportunities for Disabled People, the Arts Council, Hammersmith Hospital Arts Committee, Shape London and the London Borough of

Artwork by Giles Carey, Aycliffe Hospital. Photograph: Keith

Hammersmith and Fulham, with support from the King's Fund and the London Arts Board, and included a professional fee and materials allowance for the artist.

Nancy Willis, who trained at North-east London Polytechnic (now University), was selected from a large number of applicants. With extensive experience as a teacher and workshop leader through her work with Shape (see page 58) and in adult education, she works in two and three dimensions using different media including wood,

Nancy Willis in her studio, Hammersmith Hospital. Photographs: Gina Glover/PADT

bronze, print, clay and paint. She frequently portrays herself, representing her experience as a disabled woman.

Willis began her residency in October 1990. An old linen room situated off a busy ground floor corridor was transformed into a large studio. The space, which has good natural light, was refurbished by the hospital works department, and fitted with track and spot lighting, low-level sink and benches, and well-positioned light switches and telephone, specific to Willis's requirements. An electric wheelchair was provided by the Disabled Living Foundation for use at the studio, and a rota of designated staff devised to assist Nancy during the day.

By way of introducing herself to the hospital and to launch the residency, an exhibition of her work was held in the studio, and an edition of a self-portrait etching was made available for sale, proceeds from which offset the costs involved.

In February 1991, print-making demonstrations and workshops were held at the studio providing opportunity for hospital staff, patients and visitors to learn about Willis's work by working alongside her on a piece of their own. Posters inviting people to come along were placed around the hospital.

Professional printmaker, Caroline Coode, facilitated the workshops and assisted Willis in using and demonstrating equipment and techniques to the many people who attended, from doctors and other medical staff to patients and their relatives, several of whom came on a regular basis.

The studio is located close to the neonatal and care of the elderly units, and Willis quickly became interested in making a work about these two opposite, yet similar, stages of life when people are very fragile. As a result of seeing Willis's initial drawings made on the neonatal ward, the parentcraft sister approached her to make five drawings of mothers and babies to illustrate a hospital publication on breastfeeding. These drawings fuelled Willis's evolving ideas for her major commissioned piece for the hospital. In December 1991, final designs for this work were completed and models of these were put on display behind glass cases mounted on the wall of a main corridor, where they quickly prompted positive responses from passers-by.

Artists Agency

Aycliffe Hospital in County Durham, a long-stay hospital for people with learning difficulties, has been the setting for a permanent Artists Agency (see page 59) project since 1984. Initially begun as an artist-in-residence pilot scheme co-funded by the hospital and Northern Arts, the hospital has now completely taken over its funding and management. The district general manager of Darlington Health Authority believes the project "has demonstrated a measurable improvement in the quality of life enjoyed by those ... who have participated in (it)".

Giles Carey is a visual artist who completed a two-year residency (with further extensions) at Aycliffe. Studio space made available provided a completely different environment from that of the hospital for both himself and residents to work in. A key aim of his residency was to encourage people to make their own decisions, including whether or not to participate. An exhibition of earlier results of their work went on show at Middlesbrough Art Gallery in 1991 and featured drawings, ceramic reliefs and sculpture.

Artist placements initiated by Artists Agency at Sunderland's Cherry Knowle Psychiatric Hospital in 1984 have resulted in the creation of permanent features such as a mural for the hospital chapel, another for the swimming pool, and a rolling programme of exhibitions along corridor walls. A studio has been set up on site to enable residents to work alongside practising artists.

Another studio, The Art Studio (see page 34), was originally set up by Artists Agency as a placement for two artists to work with ex-patients of Cherry Knowle and is now an independent focus for art activity in the area.

Earls House Hospital, Durham

Earls House won the English Estates Youth Culture Award and the Astra Arts Award in 1991 for "the hospital project which has shown the most imaginative use of visual arts". The hospital has a thriving arts programme run by co-ordinator Gwyneth Lamb as part of Durham Community Health Service. This gives residents access to the arts through performances and participatory workshops.

Residents and artists Steve Marshall (of Artscope – see page 62) and Romey Chaffer painted "The Garden", a large-scale mural, for the outside wall of the activity unit in 1990, and during the following summer, at the request of the hospital's environmental committee, they painted a bottle bank with a countryside scene and a re-cycling message. The environmental theme runs through much of the arts programme and wind banners made by residents and displayed among trees in the hospital grounds exemplify this.

Project Ability

Project Ability (see page 32) has been involved in a number of projects in hospitals, frequently working with people with mental health problems and people with learning difficulties. In 1990, a group of men with mental health problems from Florence Street Day Hospital, Glasgow, and adults with learning difficulties from local training centres worked together to create large-scale clay warrior figures for public siting in Pollok Park, Glasgow. The enthusiasm and ability demonstrated was such that a follow-up six-month project in sculptural portraiture was set up in 1991 which subsequently won the 1992 Astra Award for arts projects in the mental health field.

Project Ability has now developed a hospital arts programme, Art On Wards.

Shape Projects in Hospitals

Shape London runs a regular programme of hospital art projects, which has included six months of visual arts and music workshops run by three artists at Claybury Psychiatric Hospital and a six-month drama and music project with children at St Bartholomew's Hospital, London.

In 1991, it established a six-month residency for a disabled artist at St Luke's psychiatric hospital in Muswell Hill, north London. It appointed black deaf artist Trevor Landell, who has an MA(Hons) in fine art from the Royal College of Art. A Deaf Awareness Training course for all staff, including doctors and nurses, was arranged as a start to the residency in July. Led by Laraine Callow (see page 49) and Paul Redfern, it aimed to facilitate communication with the artist and establish a rapport.

Landell ran weekly workshops with residents of three wards, producing his own work alongside their self-portraits, dreamscapes, and group collage, and later, three-colour silkscreen printing on fabric. Work by all participants went on permanent display in the hospital towards the end of the residency, and Landell led several guided tours around the exhibition, explaining using a sign interpreter how it was developed.

The case studies described here represent only a sample of the hundreds of noteworthy initiatives happening around the country which prioritise the needs and wishes of disabled people and seek to alter their cultural and social status. As this book goes to print there are many more being developed. All share the aim of achieving quality and equality of practice and experience throughout the arts.

Afterword by Sandy Nairne,
Director of Visual Arts, Arts Council

In 1985 the Arts Council published its first policy on Arts and Disability. In 1989 the Visual Arts department formed its first action plan on the Visual Arts and Disability and had already commissioned the major study on Photography and Disability carried out for the department, in collaboration with Shape London, by Liz Crow and Andrew Ormston. An important result of the action plan was to commission a study on examples of good practice in the wide field of visual arts and disability.

In Through the Front Door is the result of the research work carried out by Jayne Earnscliffe following that commission. It is not intended as a survey, but rather to highlight some of the excellent current work being carried out by artists and photographers with disabilities, to feature collaborations between disabled practitioners and all sorts of venues and to make better known the extraordinary and inventive solutions to improving and to developing workshop and exhibition provision. All these things need to be better known. It will not and cannot include every initiative of importance but if the book inspires imaginative and creative curatorship and administration then it will have done its work.

Jayne Earnscliffe has proved the most conscientious researcher, following (and exceeding) the brief in the assiduous pursuit of information and in her continuing consultation with disability organisations and specialist disabled advisers. I pay tribute to all her work. I should also like to thank Laura Down for developing the department's policies and co-ordinating the research project and production of this book. Her input has been invaluable. I would also like to thank Karen Felman for her design work and all the others who have worked with Jayne on the project.

reading on

Book of Alchemical Formulae by
Adam Reynolds

MAGAZINES

(see also Off the Shelf, page 29)

Ad Lib News – quarterly regional
newsletter on arts and disability and
disability arts. Published by Artshare
Avon. Available from: Artshare Avon,
The Yard, 6 Somerville Road, St
Andrews, Bristol BS7 9AA
(0272 420721/420722)

Access by Design – the only journal on
design, disability and the built environment. Published three times per annum
priced £15. Available from: Centre for
Accessible Environments (CAE), 35 Great
Smith Street, London SW1P 3BJ
(071-222 7980)

Artscene – a "what's on" listings
including arts and disability. Also available
on tape. Free. Available from: Yorkshire
and Humberside Arts, 21 Bond Street,
Dewsbury WF13 1AX (0924 455555)

Coalition – a quarterly grassroots
general disability publication with
regular arts features. Available from:
Greater Manchester Coalition of
Disabled People, Unit 33, Cariocca
Enterprise Park, 2 Hellidon Close,
Ardwick, Manchester M12 4AH
(061-273 5154)

Disability Arts in London (DAIL)
– a monthly "what's on" in disability
arts. Free to disabled individuals, £15
per annum to organisations. Available in
print, braille and on cassette. Contact:
Elspeth Morrison, DAIL, c/o Artsline
5 Crowndale Road, London NW1 1TU
(071-388 2227 – voice and minicom)

Disability Arts Magazine (DAM)
– a quarterly magazine. Available on
subscription £6 per annum for
unwaged, £12 for waged. Available
from: Disability Arts Magazine
10 Woad Lane, Great Coates,
Grimsby DN37 9NH

Disability Now (DN) – a monthly
magazine with regular arts section.
Published by the Spastics Society and
available on subscription priced £12 per
annum. Available from: 12 Park
Crescent, London W1N 4EQ

London Disability News – covers all
disability issues. Priced £3 to individuals,
£7 to organisations. Available from:
GLAD Greater London Association of
Disabled People, 336 Brixton Road,
London SW9 7AA (071-274 0107 –
voice and minicom)

Mailout – national arts magazine
focusing on community arts, disability
arts and black arts.
Free on subscription through selected
regional arts boards

Museums Journal – monthly journal
with information on museums, arts and
disability/access issues. Priced £40 per
annum. Available from: The Museums
Association, 42 Clerkenwell Close,
London EC1R OPA (071-608 2933)

The New Beacon – a monthly
magazine with regular features on the
arts. Available in print and braille.
Priced £12.10 per annum. Available
from: RNIB Customer Services,
PO Box 173, Peterborough PE2 6WS
(0345 023153)

Partnerships – covers arts and
disability, arts in old age and arts and
mental health. Free. Available from:
Artlink West Midlands, The Garage Arts
and Media Centre, 1 Hatherton Street,
Walsall WS1 1YB

Profile – twice yearly it covers arts and
disability developments in the North.
Available on cassette, in braille and in
print. Free. Available from: Equal Arts
Redleigh Library, Cuthbert Street,
Gateshead NE8 2HT (091 477 5533)

Training Matters – a quarterly bulletin.
Free. Available from: Arts and
Entertainment Training Council,
3 St Peter's Buildings, York Street,
Leeds LS9 8AJ

What's Going On? – a monthly
newsletter published by East Midlands
Arts. Free on subscription. Available
from: East Midlands Arts, Mountfields
House, Forest Road,
Loughborough, LE11 3HU

BOOKS/ARTICLES

**Access and Facilities for Disabled
People. Part M. Approved Document**
(1992 edition, DoE, HMSO) Priced £5
(inc p&p). Available from: Centre for
Accessible Environments (CAE),
35 Great Smith Street, London SW1P 3BJ
(071-222 7980) and HMSO bookshops

**Access Design Sheets. No.1 – Part M
No 3 – Access** by Stephen Thorpe
(1990). Priced £4 each (inc p&p).
Available from: Centre for Accessible
Environments (CAE), 35 Great Smith
Street, London SW1P 3BJ.
(071-222 7980)

**Access Provision: Alterations and
Extensions to Existing Public
Buildings** (1990). Priced £5.50 (inc
p&p). Available from: Centre for
Accessible Environments (CAE),
35 Great Smith Street, London SW1P 3BJ
(071-222 7980)

**Access to the Arts: A Disabled
Person's Guide to Arts in the Eastern
Region** (1991). Priced £2.50. Available
from: Eastern Arts Board, Cherry Hinton
Hall, Cherry Hinton Road, Cambridge
CB1 4DW (0223 215355 voice,
0223 412031 minicom 9am–5pm)

After Attenborough (1988).
Priced £2.95 (inc p&p). Available from:
Carnegie (UK) Trust, Comley Park
House, Dunfermline, Fife KY12 7EJ
(0383 721445)

Artists Newsletter – disability
supplement (June 1992 issue). Available
from: AN Publications, PO Box 23,
Sunderland SR4 6DG (091-567 3589)

Arts and Disability Action Pack
(1985, ACGB). Free. Available from:
Information Unit, The Arts Council,
14 Great Peter Street, London SW1P 3NQ
(071-333 0100)

Arts and Disability Checklist (1989,
ACGB). A quick reference guide for arts
officers on arts and disability issues.
Free. Available from: Information Unit,
The Arts Council 14 Great Peter Street,
London SW1P 3NQ (071-333 0100)

Arts and Disability Resource Pack
(1985, ACGB). Free. Available from:
Information Unit, The Arts Council,
14 Great Peter Street, London SW1P 3NQ
(071-333 0100)

**Arts and Equality: An Action Pack for
Arts Organisations** by Christine S.
Jackson (1989, Arts Development
Association). Priced £9.95. Available in
print from: Anne-Marie Doulton,
Directory of Social Change, 169 Queen's
Crescent, London NW5 4DS
(071-284 4365)

**Arts for Everyone: Guidance on
Provision for Disabled People** by
Anne Pearson (1985, Carnegie UK
Trust/CEH) Priced £7 (inc p&p).
Available from: Centre for Accessible
Environments (CAE), 35 Great Smith
Street, London SW1P 3BJ
(071-222 7980)

**Code of Practice on the Employment
of Disabled People** (1990, The
Employment Service). Available from:
Rockingham House, 123 West Street,
Sheffield S11 4ER

**Computers and Accessories for
People with Disabilities** (1991,
Disabled Living Foundation).
Priced £3.75

**The Creatures Time Forgot:
Photography and the Construction
of Disability Imagery** by David Hevey
(1992, Routledge). Priced £14.95
paperback. Recommended

Cutting the Ties That Bind by Mary
Duffy in *Feminist Arts News*, Vol. 2, No.
10, Spring 1989

Disabled Lives by Jenny Moris (1992,
BBC Educational Development and
Information). Free. Available in large
print, braille and on tape from: Disabled
Lives, PO Box 7, London W3 6XJ

Disabled Lives Difference and
Defiance. (July edition) The New
Internationalist £1.50 from The New
Internationalist, 120-126 Lavender
Avenue, Mitcham, Surrey CR4 3HP

**Directory of Museums with Facilities
for Visually Handicapped People**
(1989, RNIB). Free. Available from:
RNIB, 224 Great Portland Street,
London W1N 6AA (071-388 1266)

**Disability Arts: The Real Missing
Culture** in *Feminist Arts News*, Vol. 2,
No. 10, 1989

Disability Awareness Training
Available from: Shape London,
1 Thorpe Close, London W10 5XL
(081-960 9245)

Disability Culture: It's a Way of Life
by Sian Vasey. In *Feminist Arts News*,
Vol. 2, No. 10, Spring 1989

**Disability Equality in the Classroom:
A Human Rights Issue** by Richard
Reiser and Micheline Mason (1992,
second edition) Recommended.
Available from: Disability Equality in
Education, 78 Mildmay Grove,
London N1 4PJ

Disabled People are Everywhere. Let Us In! (1989) Available from: Artshare South West, Exeter and Devon Arts Centre, Gandy Street, Exeter EX4 3LS

Disabled People in Britain and Discrimination: A case for anti-discrimination legislation by Colin Barnes (1991, BCODP Publications) Available in print (paperback), large print, braille and tape. Priced £11.25. Recommended

Eliminating Shadows: Manual on Photography and Disability by Ray Cooper and Ronald Cooper (1991). Available in large print, paperback. Priced £12.95. Recommended. Available from: London Print Workshop, 421 Harrow Road, London W10 4RD (081-969 3247)

Environmental Equipment for Hearing Impaired People (1990) Priced £5.50 (inc p&p). Available from: Centre for Accessible Environments (CAE), 35 Great Smith Street, London SW1P 3BJ (071-222 7980)

Equal Opportunities Policy and Practice – Disability by Elspeth Morrison (1991) Priced £1.00. Recommended. Available from: Independent Theatre Council, 4 Baden Place, Crosby Row, London SE1 1YW (071-403 1727)

Frida: A Biography of Frida Kahlo by Hayden Herrera (1983, Harper and Row) Priced £8.95. Recommended

Frida Kahlo: The Paintings by Hayden Herrera (1991, Bloomsbury) Priced £25

Frieze Issue 2 1992. Naked Truth by Brian Jenkins. Available from: Frieze, 21 Denmark Street, London WC2H 8NE (071-379 1533)

Good Loo Design Guide (for public buildings) by Stephen Thorpe (1988) Priced £7 (inc p&p). Available from: Centre for Accessible Environments (CAE), 35 Great Smith Street, London SW1P 3BJ (071-222 7980)

Handshapes. A Guide to Using Sign Language Interpreters in the Arts (1990) Priced £5 (inc p&p). Available from: Shape London, 1 Thorpe Close, London W10 5XL (081-960 9245)

Historic Buildings: Accessibility and/or Conservation? (1990) Priced £5.50 (inc p&p). Available from: Centre for Accessible Environments, (CAE), 35 Great Smith Street, London SW1P 3BJ (071-222 7980)

In Search of a Heroine: Images of Women with Disabilities in Fiction and Drama by Adrienne Asch and Michelle Fine in *Women with Disabilities: Essays in Psychology, Culture and Politics* (1988, Temple University Press)

The Last Civil Rights Movement by Diane Driedger (1989, Hurst)

Learning About Self-Advocacy (The LASA pack) Priced £14.50. Available from: VIA Publications, 5 Kentings, Comberton, Cambridge CB3 7DT

A List of Audio Frequency Induction Loop Installers Available from: RNID, 105 Gower Street, London WC1E 6AH (071-387 8033)

Living Proof: Views of a World Living with HIV and AIDS. Photography and Writings (Artist's Agency) Priced £10.00. Recommended. Available from: Artists Agency, 18 Norfolk Street, Sunderland, Tyne and Wear SR1 1EA

Making Training Accessible (1991, (NCVO) Available from: NCVO Special Training Needs Taskforce, Regents Wharf 8, All Saints Street, London N1 9RL (071-713 6161)

Making Ways: The Visual Artist's Guide to Surviving and Thriving edited by David Butler and Richard Padwick (1992, third edition, AN Publications) Priced £11.95

Means of Escape for Disabled People: BS 5588 Part 8 (1992) Priced £7.00 (inc p&p). Available from: Centre for Accessible Environments (CAE), 35 Great Smith Street, London SW1P 3BJ (071-222 7980)

More Than Ramps Available from: NALGO, 1 Mabledon Place, London WC1H 9AJ (071-388 2366)

Museums Without Barriers by Fondation de France/ICOM (1991, Routledge) Priced £20

A Natural History of the Senses by Diane Ackerman (1990, Chapmans) Priced £6.99

Off the Shelf and Into Action / ACGB Arts and Disability Directory (1991) Available in large print, braille and tape. Free to disabled people and to disability organisations. Arts organisations can obtain it for £7 ring bound, £5 spiral bound. Other organisations, £12 and £10 respectively. Recommended. Available from: Information Unit, The Arts Council, 14 Great Peter Street, London SW1P 3NQ (071-333 0100)

On Our Own Behalf – an Introduction to the Self-Organisation of Disabled People by Martin Pagel (1988, Greater Manchester Coalition of Disabled People)

Organising Your Exhibition by Debbie Duffin (1991, second edition) Priced £7.25. Recommended. Available from: AN Publications PO Box 23, Sunderland SR4 6DG (091-567 3589)

Out of Sight: The Experience of Disability 1900–1950 (1992) Priced £10.99. Available from: Northcote House Publishers, Estover Road, Plymouth PL6 7PZ

Photography and Disability in England: A Report Commissioned by ACGB and Shape London (1990, ACGB) Free. Available from: Information Unit, The Arts Council, 14 Great Peter Street, London SW1P 3NQ (071-333 0100)

Places That Care –- The Access Guide to Places of Interest Suitable for Elderly and Disabled People compiled by M. Yarrow. Priced £4.99. Available from: Mediair Marketing Services, 72 High Street, Poole, Dorset BH15 1DA

Play, Arts and Leisure Activities for Disabled Children, Their Parents and Carers Free. Available from: Artsline, 5 Crowndale Road, London NW1 1TU (071-388 2227 voice and minicom)

The Politics of Disablement by Mike Oliver (1990, Macmillan) Priced £8.95

Pride Against Prejudice – Transforming Attitudes to Disability by Jenny Morris (1991, The Women's Press) Priced £6.95. Recommended

Reading Plans: A Layman's Guide to the Interpretation of Architect's Drawings by Stephen Thorpe (1986 Access Committee for England) Priced £6.50. Available from: Centre for Accessible Environments (CAE), 35 Great Smith Street, London SW1P 3BJ (071-222 7980)

A Sense of Self – Bodies of Experience: Stories about Living with HIV (1989 Camerawork/The Photo Co-op) Priced £4.50. Available from: Camerawork, 121 Roman Road, London E2 0QN (081-980 6256)

Smashing Icons: Disabled Women and the Disability and Women's Movement by Adrienne Asch and Michelle Fine from *Women with Disabilities: Essays in Psychology, Culture and Politics* (1988, Temple University Press)

Social Work: Disabled People and Disabling Environments edited by Michael Oliver (Jessie Kingsley Publishers) Priced £17.95

Supporting Self-Advocacy edited by Andrea Whittaker. Priced £6.50. Available from: Bailey Distribution Ltd, Dept KFP, Learoyd Road, Mountfield Industrial Estate, New Romney, Kent TN28 8XU

They Aren't in the Brief by Susan Scott-Parker (1989) Available from: King's Fund Centre, 126 Albert Street, London NW1 7NF

Touching the Rock: An Experience of Blindness by John Hull (1990, Arrow) Priced £4.99. Recommended

Working Together for Access: A Manual for Access Groups (1991) Available in print, braille and on tape. Priced £7.00 (inc p&p). Available from: Publications Section, Access Committee for England, 35 Great Smith Street, London SW1P 3BJ (071-233 2566)

Women's Art Magazine No. 47, July / August 1992 Art, Health & Disability. Available from: The Women Artists. Slide Library, Fulham Palace, Bishops Avenue, London SW6 6EA (071-731 7618)

The World Through Blunted Sight by Patrick Trevor-Roper (1990, Penguin) Priced £9.99

contacts

Access Committee for England
35 Great Smith Street, London SW1P
3BJ (071-233 2566)

Access Committee for Wales
Ilys Ifor Crescent Road, Caerphilly CF8
1XL (0222 887 325)

ADAPT
45 Harrington Gardens,
London SW7 4JU (071-373 8121)
Contact: Derek Lodge

Age Concern Astral House, 1268
London Road, London SW16 4ER
(081-679 8000)

AIRS Gateshead Central Library,
Prince Consort Road, Gateshead NE8
4LN (091-477 3478)

All Clear Designs 107 The Chandlery,
50 Westminster Bridge Road, London
SE1 7QY (071-721 7480)

The Ark South Hill Park Arts Centre,
Bracknell RG12 4PA (0344 483311)

Artists Agency 18 Norfolk Street,
Sunderland SR1 1EA (091-510 9318)

Artlink Edinburgh and the Lothians
13a Spittal Street, Edinburgh EH3 9DY
(031-229 3555)

Artlink West Yorkshire 191 Belle
Vue Road, Leeds LS3 1HG
(0532 431005)

Arts Access 15 New Bridge Street,
London EC4 6AU

Arts Access (Arts in Education
Advisory Agency) 40 High Street,
Berkeley GL13 9BJ (0453 810488)

Arts Connection Cumberland Centre,
Reginald Road, Portsmouth PO4 9HN
(0705 828392)

Artscope 24 Douglas Gardens,
Dunston, Gateshead, Tyne and Wear
NE11 9RA
(091-413 5340 – Malcolm Smith)
(091-460 4662 – Steve Marshall)

Arts Council 14 Great Peter Street,
London SW1P 3NQ (071-333 0100)

Arts Council of Northern Ireland
181a Stranmills Road Belfast, BT9 5DU
(0232 381591)

Artshare Avon The Yard, 6 Somerville
Road, St Andrews, Bristol BS7 9AA
(0272 420721/420722)

Arts in Fife Markinch Centre, Bowling
Green Road, Markinch KY7 6BD
(0592 756633)

Artsline 5 Crowndale Road, London
NW1 1TU (071-388 2272– voice and
minicom)

Artsreach Jacksons Lane Community
Centre, 269a Archway Road, London
N6 5AA (081-340 5226)

Arts Special Info 63 Hillhead Street,
Glasgow G12 8QF (041-330 4925)
Contact: Josephine Gammell

The Art Studio 1/3 Hind Street,
Sunderland SR1 3QD (091-567 7414)

Art to Share c/o Rachel Jones,
3 Orston Green, Wollaton Park,
Nottingham NG8 LAH (0602 598835)

**Asian People with Disabilities
Alliance** Ground Floor, Willesden
Hospital, Harlesden Road, London
NW10 3RY (081-459 5793)

**Association for Business
Sponsorship for the Arts (ABSA)**
Nutmeg House, 60 Gainsford Street,
Butler's Wharf, London SE1 2NY
(071-378 8143)

**Association for the Promotion of
Disabled Artists** Blumenauer Strasse
9, D-3000, Hannover 91, Germany
(010 49/5 11/45 40 51)

Avon Coalition of Disabled People
c/o 81 Valentine Close, Whitchurch,
Bristol, Avon

Battersea Arts Centre Old Town Hall,
Lavender Hill, London SW11 5TF
(071-223 6557)

Black Disabled People's Group
336 Brixton Road, London SW9 7AA
(071-274 0107)

**British Council of Organisations of
Disabled People (BCODP)**
De Bradelei House, Chapel Street,
Belper DE56 1AR
(0773 828182 – voice)
(0773 828195 – minicom)

British Deaf Association 38 Victoria
Place, Carlisle CA1 1HU
(0228 28719 – qwerty phone)
(0228 48844 – voice/minicom)

British Museum Education Service
Great Russell Street, London WC1 3DG
(071-323 8327)

Camerawork 121 Roman Road,
Bethnal Green, London E2 0QN
(081-980 6256)

Carousel 2 St Georges Place, Brighton
BN1 4GB (0273 570840)

Centre for Accessible Environments
35 Great Smith Street, London SW1P
3BJ (071-222 7980)

Chats Palace 42–44 Brooksby Walk,
Hackney, London E91 6DF
(081-533 0227)

Community Arts Workshop Unit 5,
Daisy Bank Industrial Estate, Stockport
Road, Longsight, Manchester M13 0LF
(061-273 7964)

CRAB Tedder Studios, Wiggins Mead,
Off Cornermead, Grahame Park Way,
Hendon, London NW9 5UD
(081-200 8353)

Department of the Environment
2 Marsham Street, London SW1 P3EB
(071-276 3000)

**Derbyshire Coalition of Disabled
People** 117 High Street, Clay Cross,
Chesterfield (0246 865305)

Directory of Social Change
169 Queen's Crescent, London NW5 4DS
(071-284 4365)

Disability Alliance First Floor East,
Universal House, 88–94 Wentworth
Street, London E1 75A (071-274 8776)

Disabled Drivers Association Drake
House, 18 Creekside, London SE8 3DZ

Disabled Living Foundation
380 Harrow Road, London W9 2HU
(071-289 6111)

The Disabled Photographers Society
PO Box 130, Richmond TW10 6XQ

East End Arts Access 64 Tollcross
Road, Glasgow G31 4XE
(041-554 6253)

Eastern Arts Cherry Hinton Hall,
Cherry Hinton Road, Cambridge
CB1 4DW (0223 215355)

Echo City c/o Giles Perring,
229 Pemberton Terrace,
Upper Holloway, London N19 5RY
(071-263 9153)

Equal Arts Redheugh Library,
Cuthbert Street, Gateshead NE8 2HT
(091-477 5533)

Format 19 Arlington Way, Islington,
London EC1R 1UY (071-833 0292)

Foundation for Sport and the Arts
PO Box 666, Liverpool L69 7JN
(051-524 0235/6) Contact: Grattan
Endicott, secretary

Gateshead Libraries and Arts
Central Library, Prince Consort Road,
Gateshead NE8 4LN
(091-477 3478/3842)

The Genesis Project
171/175 Upper Hanover Street,
Broomhall, Sheffield S3 7RR
(0742 755510)

**Greater London Association of
Disabled People (GLAD)**
336 Brixton Road, London SW9 7AA
(071-274 0107 – voice and minicom)

Glasgow Forum on Disability
Room 21, 1st Floor McIver House
51 Cadogen Street, Glasgow G2 7QB
(041-227 6125)

**Greater Manchester Coalition of
Disabled People**
Unit 33, Cariocca Enterprise Park,
2 Hellidon Close, Ardwick
Manchester M12 4AH (061-273 5154)

Greenwich Citizens Gallery
151 Powis Street, Woolwich, London
SE18 6JL (081-316 2752)

Grizedale Sculpture Trail Theatre in
the Forest, Grizedale, Hawkshead
Ambleside LA22 0QJ
(0229 860291)
Contact: Bill Grant, Director

Harris Museum & Art Gallery
Market Square, Preston PR1 2PP
(0772 58248)

Havant Arts Centre Old Town Hall,
East Street, Havant PO9 1BS
(0705 472700)

Hereward College Bramston Crescent,
Tile Hill Lane, Coventry CV4 9SW
(0203 461231)

Horse and Bamboo Foundry Street,
Rawtenstall, Rossendale BB4 6HQ
(0706 220241)

Ikon Gallery 58–72 John Bright Street,
Birmingham B1 1BN (021-643 0708)

In-Valid? Community Arts Centre,
The Old Quaker School, 17–21 Chapel
Street, Bradford BD1 5DJ
(0274 721372)

Key Gallery 2 Queens Crescent, St Georges Cross, Glasgow G4 9BW (041-332 4632)

William Kirby (Consultant in art and design for blind and partially sighted people), Eastgate Street, Winchester SO23 8EB (0962 854003)

Leeds City Art Galleries Temple Newsam House, Leeds LS15 0AE (0532 647321)

Living Paintings Trust Silchester Hse, Silchester, Nr Reading RG7 2LT (0734 700 776) Contact: Alison Oldland

London Arts Board 133 Long Acre, London WC2E 9AF (071-240 1313)

The London Boroughs Disability Resource Team (LBDRT) 1st Floor Bedford House, 125-133 Camden High Street, London NW1 7JR (071-482 4896)

London Disability Arts Forum (LDAF) The Diorama, 14 Peto Place, London NW1 (071-935 5588/8999 – voice) (071-935 8999 – minicom)

London Print Workshop 421 Harrow Road, London W10 4RD (081-969 3247)

Milton Keynes Council of Disabled People City Square, 536 Silbury Blvd, Central Milton Keynes, MK9 3AF

Minorities Arts Advisory Service (MAAS) Fourth Floor,28 Shacklewell Lane, London E8 2EZ (071-254 7239/7295)

The Mix The Neighbourhood Centre, 42 Church Lane, London N2 9PJ (081-883 2832)

Museums and Galleries Commission 16 Queen, Anne's Gate, London SW1H 9AA (071-233 4200)

Museums and Galleries Disabilities Association (MAGDA) c/o City Art Gallery, Mosley Street, Manchester M2 3JL (061-236 5244 ext 123)

Museum Science and Industry Liverpool Road, Castlefield, Manchester M3 4JP (061-832 2244)

National Advisory Council on Employment of People with Disabilities The Employment Dept. SEPC3, Level 1 Caxton House, Tothill Street, London SW1H 9NF (071-273 6018 NACRD Secretariat)

National Disability Arts Forum Katherine Walsh, Secretary c/o West Midlands Council for Disabled People, Moseley Hall Hospital, Birmingham B1 38JL

National League of the Blind and Disabled (recognised trade union) 2 Tenterden Road, Tottenham, London N17 8BE (081-808 6030)

National League of the Deaf/Blind 18 Rainbow Court, Paston Ridings, Peterborough PE4 7UP (0733 573511)

National Star Centre Ullenwood Cheltenham, GL53 9QU (0242 527631)

Northern Ireland Disabilities Forum 105 Botanic Gardens, Belfast BT7 1NN

Northern Ireland Regional Access Committee 2 Annadale Avenue, Belfast B77 3JH

North West Disability Arts Forum (NWDAF) 2a Franceys Street, Off Brownlow Hill, Liverpool L3 (081-707 1733)

North West Shape Back of Shawgrove School, Cavendish Road, West Didsbury Manchester M20 8JR (061-434 8666)

Nottinghamshire Coalition of Disabled People 32a Park Row Nottingham NG1 6GR (0602 475531)

NUBS Interchange Trust, 15 Wilkin Street, London NW5 3NQ (071-267 9421)

Open Arts 105 Botanic Avenue, Belfast BT7 1NN (0232 245133 ext 3580) Contact: Kate Ingram, project officer

Opportunities for Disabled People 1 Bank Buildings, Princes Street, London EC2R 8EU (071-726 4961)

People First (self-advocacy organisation of people with learning difficulties) Instrument House, 207-215 Kings Cross Road, London WC1 9DB (071-713 6400)

Project Ability 18 Albion Street, Glasgow G1 1LH (041-552 2822)

Public Art Development Trust 1a Cobham Mews, Agar Grove, London NW1 9SB (071-284 4983)

Raku Works Sculptural Arts Mercer House, Mercer Park, Clayton-le-Moors, Accrington BB5 5NZ (0254 391412)

REGARD (organisation of disabled lesbians and gay men), c/o 88 Maidstone Road, London N11 2JR

Royal National Institute for Deaf People 105 Gower Street, London WC1E 6AH (071 387 8033/3154 – minicom)

Royal National Institute for Disability and Rehabilitation (RADAR) 25 Mortimer Street, London W1N 8AB (071-637 5400)

Royal National Institute for the Blind 224 Great Portland Street, London W1A 6AA (071-388 1266)

Scottish Art Council 112 Manor Place, Edinburgh EH3 7DD (031-226 6051)

Shape London 1 Thorpe Close, London W10 5XL (081-960 9245)

START Studios High Elms, Upper Park Road, Victoria Park, Manchester M14 5RU (061-276 6345)

Stoke City Museum and Art Gallery Hanley, Stoke-on-Trent ST1 3DW (0782 202173)

Survivors Speak Out (self-help group of people who have been diagnosed as mentally ill) 33 Lichfield Road, London NW2 2RG (081-450 4631)

Tate Gallery Albert Dock, Liverpool L3 4BB (051-709 3223)

Tullie House, Carlisle City Museum and Art Gallery Castle Street, Carlisle CA3 8TP (0228 34781)

University of Northumbria at Newcastle Arts Management Centre, Squires Building, Sandyford Road, Newcastle upon Tyne NE1 8ST (091-235 8920)

Valley and Vale Blaengarw Workmen's Hall, Blaengarw, Bridgend, Mid Glamorgan CF32 8AW (0656 871911)

Voluntary Organisations Communications and Language (VOCAL) 336 Brixton Road, London W9 7AA (071-274 4029)

Whitechapel Art Gallery 80–82 Whitechapel High Street, London E1 7QX (071-377 0107)

Win Visible (Women with Visible and Invisible Disabilities) Kings Cross Women's Centre, 71 Tonbridge Street, London WC1H 9DZ (071-837 7509)

Yorkshire Sculpture Park Bretton Hall, West Bretton, Wakefield WF4 4LG (0924 830579)

PROGRAMMES AND SERVICES

No Need to Shout BBC1 and BBC2 Ceefax, Chas Donaldson, PO Box 701, Glasgow G42 9XG (041-632 0024)

Earshot Channel 4 Oracle, c/o Charles Herd, 22 Carlton Green, Redhill, Surrey RH1 2DA

Into the Arena Arts programme produced by the BBC's Disability Programme Unit scheduled for screening summer 1993. It will cover disabled people's art and mainstream arts events reviewed by disabled reporters.

From the Edge BBC2 A series of reports on the arts, politics and news from disabled reporters. Edited by Karena Marchant with sign language interpretation

Link ITV Central Sunday mornings

See Hear! BBC1

Sign Extra BBC1

In Touch BBC Radio 4 FM, Tuesdays

Does He Take Sugar BBC Radio 4 FM

Sign On Channel 4, Tyne Tees TV, City Road, Newcastle upon Tyne NE1 2AL (091-261 1922 – voice and minicom)

Typetalk National telephone relay service launched June 1991 by RNID and British Telecom. Operates 24 hours every day of the year and allows deaf, partially deaf and speech impaired people to communicate with hearing people throughout the world via the public telephone (minicom).

National Telephone Relay Service Pauline Ashley House Ravenside Retail Park, Speke Road, Liverpool L24 8QB (051-494 100 – voice) (051-494 1085 – minicom)

For details on minicom contact: **Electronic Communications Group** RNID 105 Gower Street London, WC1 6AH (071-387 8033 – voice) (071-383 3154 – minicom)

acknowledgements   index

My thanks to Margaret Mannion, Access Committee for England; Edward Adamson, Adamson Collection; Derek Lodge, ADAPT; Maggie Goodbarn, AIRS; Vicky Waddington and James Holmes-Siedle, All Clear; Susan Jones, Richard Padwick, Lynn Evans and Sharon McKee, AN Publications; Penny Sanderson, The Ark; Armley Centre; Archæological Resource Centre, York; Michael Archer, artist; Stephen Snoddy, formerly of the Arnolfini; Art-ic-u-late; Lucy Milton and Esther Salamon, Artists Agency; Pauline Eyre, Artlink East; Sarah Munro, Brenda Smith and Jan-Bert Van Den Berg, Artlink Edinburgh and the Lothians; David Mudge, Artlink Lincolnshire and Humberside; Pat Taylor, Artlink Oxon; Karen Wilson, Artlink Staffs; Cynth Hopkin and Andrea Lamb, Artlink West Yorkshire; Peter Cooper, Arts Access; Julian and Liz Davies, Arts Access, Berkeley; Lynne Dick, Lynn Legge and Richard Wiczkowski, Arts Connection; Steve Marshall and Malcolm Smith, Artscope; Primrose Finigan, Arts Council of Northern Ireland; Rhian Davies, Arts for Disabled People in Wales; Jo Doyle, Artshare Avon; Magnus More, Andrew Neil and Gillian McFarland, Arts in Fife; Val Stein, Artsline; Pat Place, Artsreach; Nicky Wynne, Derek Hill and Chris Sell, The Art Studio; Rachel and Lewis Jones, Art to Share; Stephanie Ash, access worker; Emma Ayling, artist/photographer; Suzie Balazs, artist; Anna Parker, Barbican; Chris Reid and Josephine Wilson (Shape), Battersea Arts Centre; Peter Harris, Beaford Centre; Millie Hill, Black Disabled People's Group; Sally Booth, artist; John Elsworth, Braille Unit, Leeds Central Library; Peter Howell, Brighton Cathedrals Through Touch and Hearing Project; Brighton Museum; Hilary Woolley, Bristol City Museum and Art Gallery; Malcolm Miles, British Health Care Arts; Anne Pearson, British Museum; Karen Cornwall, British Petroleum; Cambridge Darkroom; Dawn Langley, formerly of Camerawork; Dick Capel; Laura Guthrie and Julie Lancaster, Carnegie (UK) Trust; Carousel; Tessa Palfreyman and Andrew Lacey, Centre for Accessible Environments; Cleveland Gallery; Laura Hamilton, Collins Gallery; Margaret Williams, Commonwork; Wendy Parry and Neil Payne, Community Arts Workshop; Ursula Hulme, Conquest; Caroline Coode, print-maker; Gordon Cooper, photographer; Dewi Lewis, Cornerhouse; Counter Image; Maria Bartha and Priscilla Judd, CRAB; Elspeth Morrison, DAIL; Laurence Ward, Darlington Arts Centre; Laraine Callow, Deafworks; Dean Clough; Hazel Moffat, Department of Education and Science; Diorama; Robert Pickles, Disability Scotland; Peter Stroud, Disabled Photographers' Society; Mary Duffy; Gillian Wolfe, Dulwich Picture Gallery; Gwyneth Lamb, Earls House Hospital Arts; Frances Grant, East End Arts Access; Annie Delin, East Midlands Arts; François Matarasso, East Midlands Shape; Giles Perring, Echo City; Tracy Warr, Edge; Mr Cootes, Edinburgh District Council; Frances O'Brien (and Sue Roberts formerly of), Equal Arts; Julie Flack; Alan Counsell, Focus Disability;Forkbeard Fantasy; Format; William Forrester, access consultant; Caroline Foxhall, formerly of Ikon; Josephine Gammell, Arts Special Info; Lucy Gampell, formerly of Shape East; Mike White and Anna Pepperall, Gateshead Libraries and Arts; Jan Swain, The Genesis Project; Donna Jackman-Wilson, GLAD; Glasgow Art Centre; Selwyn Goldsmith, DoE; Greater Manchester Coalition of Disabled People; Val Green, formerly of Matrix; Lesley Greene; Greenwich Citizens Gallery; Bill Grant, Grizedale Theatre in the Forest; Gunnersbury Park Museum; Raina Haig; Alex Walker and Brian Manning, Harris Museum and Art Gallery; Paul Sadler, Havant Art Centre; Hayward Gallery; Sue Ball, Hertfordshire College of Art and Design; Alison Bowrey, High Peak Community Arts; Horniman Museum; Bob Frith and Melissa Wier, Horse and Bamboo; Guy Eades, Hospital Arts, I.O.W; Huddleston Centre; Bridget Roseberry and Catherine Ugwu, ICA; IDEA; Liz Anne McGregor and Angela Kingston, Ikon; Impressions Gallery; Inter-Action, MK; Interchange; Ruth Collett and Ruth Malkin, In-Valid; Brendon Duffy, Irvine Development Corporation; Kendal Museum; Sarah Derrick, Kettle's Yard; Ian Hamilton and Mansell Griffiths, Key Gallery; William Kirby, art consultant; Jason Kirk, Laing Gallery; Lavengro Print, north London; Sian Vasey, LDAF; Adam White, Leeds City Art Galleries; Leicester Museum; Rachel Sullivan, Leicester University; Living Paintings Trust; Llanover Hall Arts Centre; London Boroughs' Disability Resource Team; John Phillips, London Print Workshop; Peter Macdonald, photo-journalist; MAGDA; Pauline Webb, Manchester Museum of Science and Industry; David Mansell, The Observer; Peter McDonald, poet; Ann Barrett, Medway Arts Centre; Mencap; Willy Milne, formerly of Kendal Museum; MIND; Makeda Coaston, Minorities Arts Advisory Service; Milton Keynes Exhibitions Gallery; The Mix; Tony Lumley, Mobility International; MOMA, Oxford; More Balls Than Most; Carolyn Keen and Chris Newbery, Museums and Galleries Commission; Museum of Garden History; Museum of London; Christine Jackson, NAAC; Flick Allen, NAGE; Maureen O'Mara, National Federation of Gateway Clubs; Jane Dewey, National Maritime Museum; David Finch, National Star Centre; Nottingham Castle Museum; North Western Federation of Museums and Art Galleries; Brian Hilton, North West Shape; Nelson De Silva, NUBS; Di Christian, NWDAF; Kate Ingram, Open Arts, Northern Ireland; Open Eye Gallery; Adam Sutherland, Ormond Street Workshops; Vi Hendrickson, Pavilion; Photofusion; Keith Pickard, formerly Shape Training; Portfolio Gallery; Kathleen McArthur, Project Ability; Caroline Taylor, Projects UK; Cat Newton-Groves, Public Art Development Trust; Sue Blagden, Queen Alexandra College; RADAR; Iain Cartwright, Raku Works; Samena Rana, RIBA; Marcus Weisen, RNIB; RNID; Christine Ross, formerly public art officer, Hammersmith and Fulham; John Everett, Royal National College; Royal Academy; Kirin Saeed; Derek Gillman, Sainsbury Centre for Visual Arts; Stuart Olesker, School for Continuing Education; Susan Christie, Scottish Arts Council; Scottish Arts Lobby; Sally Sedgwick; Serpentine Gallery; Ann Gabriel, Shape Bucks; Maggie Woolley, Guy Evans and Jackie Huber, Shape London; Helen Sloan, formerly of Oldham Art Gallery; Trisha Cooke-Smith Art Gallery; Lynne Greene, Southampton City Art Gallery; South Bank Centre; Frances Smith, South East Arts; Piers Benn, Southern Artlink; Jack Sutton and Langley Brown, START; Ben Steiner, artist/signer; Gioya Steinke, artist/critic; Stills Gallery; Jim Shea, Stoke City Museum and Art Gallery; Toby Jackson, Adrian Plant, Alison Blease, Tate Gallery, Liverpool; Third Eye; Stephen Thorpe, architect; Trisha Legall, TIPP; Tramway; Moira Innes, TSWA; Catherine Tucker; Andy Anderson, Ulster Folk and Transport Museum; Ulster Museum; Helen Croxhall, University of Leicester; Ian Wolfenden, University of Manchester; Untitled Gallery; Upper Springlands; Imogen Stewart, V & A; Hilary Gresty, VAGA; Phil Cope, Valley and Vale; Maggie Wirgman and Anne Louise, Waterfront; Gabby Campbell, Watermans Art Centre; The Watershed; Maureen Rooksby, West Yorkshire Playhouse; David Wextone, The Journal, Newcastle; my friends at the Whitechapel Art Gallery; Nancy Willis; Reen Pilkington, Willowbrook Urban Studies Centre; Liz Ellis, Workshops on Demand; David Wright, formerly of City Gallery Arts Trust; Debbie and Jon Wurr; Peter Murray, Yorkshire Sculpture Park.

Thanks are also due to all the arts officers at the Arts Council and Regional Arts Boards for their assistance in the initial stages of my research. My special thanks go to Sandy Nairne, director of visual arts at the Arts Council, for giving me the opportunity, space and support to take the research on to its natural conclusion; to Noelle Goldman-Jacob for her initial encouragement; and to Laura Down for her unfailing commitment.

Also many thanks to Karen Felman for her unceasing flow of creative ideas, patience and good humour; to Debbie Duffin for her professional advice; to Audrey Barker for her generosity and wisdom; and to my family and friends who didn't desert me during my labour of love.

I am indebted to Anne Marie Cavanah, Urve Opik, Mary Fenwick and Katy Heath for their invaluable assistance, to my draft readers David (comrade) Hevey, Barbara Hunt, Bushy Kelly, Sue (per ardua ad astra) Killen and Adam Reynolds, and to my copy editor, Tracey Brett, for her diplomatic changes. I would also like to extend my gratitude to Charles Pither and Phil Richardson at St Thomas's Hospital Pain Management Unit for the "shot in the arm".

Italics denote publications, exhibitions and seminars